Hugh Mackay is a psychologist and social researcher who has spent the past 40 years studying the attitudes and behaviour of the Australian community.

He was born in 1938 and educated at Sydney Grammar School, the University of Sydney and Macquarie University. In 1985, he was elected a Fellow of the Australian Psychological Society in recognition of his pioneering work in the application of qualitative methodology to social research. He is an honorary Professorial Fellow in the Graduate School of Management at Macquarie University and a former Deputy Chairman of the Australia Council.

He is the author of two bestsellers in the field of social psychology: *Reinventing Australia* (1993) and *Why Don't People Listen?* (1994). He has also written two novels, *Little Lies* (1996) and *House Guest* (1997), and writes a weekly column on social issues for the *Weekend Australian*.

Other Books by Hugh Mackay

NON-FICTION
Reinventing Australia
Why Don't People Listen?

FICTION
Little Lies
House Guest

GENERATIONS

HUGH MACKAY

MACMILLAN
Pan Macmillan Australia

First published 1997 in Macmillan by Pan Macmillan Australia Pty Limited
St Martins Tower, 31 Market Street, Sydney

National Library of Australia
Cataloguing-in-Publication data:

Mackay, Hugh.
Generations.

ISBN 0 7329 0921 X.

1. Generations – Australia. 2. Australia – Social
conditions – 20th century. 3. Australia – Social life and
customs – 20th century. I. Title.

305.20994

Typeset in 11/14 pt Sabon by Post Pre-press Group
Printed in Australia by McPherson's Printing Group

CONTENTS

INTRODUCTION

There is no mystery, except to their parents, about why generations think and act as they do. Since we all share remarkably similar genetic material, generation gaps aren't biologically inevitable: they are simply the result of different generations spending their formative years in different social, cultural, economic and technological environments. When those environments are changing rapidly, generation gaps can feel more like chasms than fissures, and the task of maintaining close relationships with people on the other side may seem very daunting.

When you're standing forlornly on the edge of the gap, wondering what happened to those open, loving, communicative and biddable creatures who used to be your children, it's not easy to console yourself with the thought that every generation adds their own momentum to the process of cultural evolution, that every generation makes a distinctive contribution to the shaping of a society – and that every older generation finds something deplorable about the young.

It's far easier for parents and other observers of young people to take refuge in the comfort of prejudice, even the prejudice that damns the rising generation with faint praise:

Of course, they're so much better educated than we were.

or keeps its distance from them by resorting to pity:

I'm glad I don't have to face the pressures they're under, what with drugs and unemployment and such a competitive environment.

They're so much smarter than we were, but they seem to lose their innocence at such an early age, don't you feel?

1

*They think in a completely different way from us. I blame the
influence of TV for a lot of it . . . and computers, of course.*

Parents can accept that the changing environment defines the cultural divide between one generation and the next as long as they
focus on safely external things like the cycles of fashion in education, the impact of computers, rock music, drugs, takeaway food or
the mass media. The argument gets a little trickier, though, when
they start to speculate about their own role in the creation of the
values, style and outlook of their children's generation.

The most powerful of the influences on most young people is the
example of their own parents. The biggest difference between your
generation and your children's generation is not likely to have been
the advent of the computer, nor the threat of AIDS, nor the level of
unemployment. It is more likely to be the fact that – for better or
worse – you had your parents for parents, and your children had you.

The values of our parents aren't transmitted to us intact:
indeed, they are sometimes utterly rejected for some years, or forever. But all those early years of living in a family run by parents
with a particular way of looking at the world inevitably affects the
way we, too, look at the world. We are always their children, and
we respond to our own world under the heavy influence of the way
they responded to theirs. As the Welsh poet and novelist D. M.
Thomas puts it: 'I can see almost nothing that I owe to [my father],
almost nothing we have in common. Yet also, at the same time, I
smile with his smile, weep with his tears.'[1]

Simply by being a parent, you have supplied an important part of
the context for your children's attempts to make sense of the world.
'Society' plays its part, of course, but it's too easy – too convenient – to
blame society for the emergence of traits in our children which we find
unattractive, and for which we'd rather not have to accept too much
responsibility. But the truth is that our way of life is the reference point
– the point of departure – for their journey towards independence.

At the end of World War II, the Australian birth rate rose to record
levels, creating the generation who came to be known as the Baby

Boomers. (They also came to be known as the Me Generation, and the story of how they earned that label is one of the themes of this book.)

By their sheer numbers, they have cut a swathe through Australian society, transforming the institutions of primary, secondary and tertiary education; creating a 'youth market' in fashion and music, and drawing attention to 'teenagers' as a distinct subculture; dramatically expanding the car market, the travel market and the leisure market; and presiding over the decline of formal religious practice.

But the real significance of the Boomers is not just that there are so many of them: it is that they disrupted the established pattern of cultural baton-passing from one generation to the next. They were – and are – a breakthrough generation. The phrase 'generation gap' was coined for them.

Biologically, a generation is measured by the time it takes an organism to reach sexual maturity: human generations have therefore been traditionally defined in 15-year spans. Colloquially, we are less strict than that: we tend to speak of generations in terms of a group of individuals who were born at about the same time, or in the same era, and who have been subject to common social, cultural and economic influences.

Some demographers use a 30-year gap to separate generations; some use 15 years, following the biological cycle. In this book, a 25-year gap has been chosen, reflecting, in round figures, the average time between a woman's birth and the birth of her first child, at least for the two older generations under review. That span – from birth to first-child's birth – is being extended as the rising generation of young adults postpone both marriage and parenthood. (In the early 1970s, when Boomers were establishing their families, the median age of mothers having their first child was 23 years; by the mid-1990s, it had risen to 29 years.)

The three generations analysed in this book have been narrowed down to ten-year spans: the generation born in the 1920s; their children's generation (the Boomers) born in the late 1940s and early 1950s; and the children of the Boomers, born in the 1970s.

Obviously, no generations fall as neatly as that. People born in the 1920s have a great deal in common with those born in the early

1930s, and the parents of Boomers are certainly not confined to those who were born in the 1920s. The Boomers themselves are generally acknowledged as being the generation born between 1946 and 1961 but, for the purposes of this analysis, we have concentrated on 'leading-edge' Boomers born in 1946–1955 (sometimes referred to as Early Boomers), since they were the real pioneers of baby-boomer culture.

The children of Boomers are still being born – especially to parents who have deliberately postponed parenthood, or those who are marrying for the second or third time. Nevertheless, the first wave of Early Boomers' offspring were born in the 1970s.

The thesis of *Generations* is that these three age groups represent three radically different phases in the development of Australian society, and that the differences between them – in attitudes, values and outlook – are therefore symbolic of significant culture shifts.

But *Generations* is not a work of social history: its goals are more modest than that. It is based primarily on a social research program, *The Mackay Report*, which is devoted to exploring the attitudes of contemporary Australians and using those attitudes as signs and symptoms of some of the ways in which patterns of life in Australia are changing. Of the 89 reports published since this project began in 1979, 15 have particularly illuminated the themes in this book and supplied the 'voices' which are heard throughout its pages. (Those 15 reports are identified in the Appendix, where the research methods used for *The Mackay Report* are also fully described.)

A problem inherent in this type of social research is that it tries to construct a big picture out of a series of miniatures. Generalisations – however tentative – have to be made and yet, in one sense, everyone is an exception because everyone's story is unique. In any case, *Generations* does not propose a Grand United Theory of generational change. It is simply an attempt to identify some of the patterns in the attitudes of three generations of Australians, and to highlight some important differences between them. It will have served its purpose if, seeing themselves reflected in these pages, members of those generations find it a little easier to understand themselves and each other.

1
THREE GENERATIONS:
THREE AUSTRALIAS?

Midway through 1997, the *Australian* published a letter from John Murphy, president-elect of Grey Power Queensland. Mr Murphy began by reminding readers that New Zealand is called the 'land of the long white cloud', and then suggested that Australia might soon be known as 'the land of the big black cloud'. After berating governments at all levels – Federal, State and local – for creating 'smokescreens' to conceal the real issues, he went on to say this:

> All these screens are being created instead of tackling the main problems of unemployment, healthcare, law and order and the general quality of Australian life. I wonder if they are clever enough to tackle them?
>
> It is interesting to note that the CSIRO National Survey found 52 per cent of our population believe the quality of life was becoming more and more eroded and only 13 per cent believed it was getting better. I must say that I agree with the 52 per cent and that it is time to 'regain the agenda' and re-install in this country the quality of living we once shared.

At his latest address in Brisbane, environmentalist Dr David Suzuki admitted he had changed his earlier opinion that the younger generation was the key to the future. He now feels that it is the elderly who need to tell the younger people just how good life and the environment really used to be. After two wars, maybe we were more content with simple pleasures – trust, friendship, caring, communication and a conviction that it was basically a kind world we were living in.

The population over 50 years of age is a major proportion of the voting public and it is time to make our vote count by standing up for these vital issues.

Personally, I look forward to the day when I can leave the doors to my home unlocked, living in contentment and harmony with my fellow human beings. Am I really hoping for too much?[1]

Towards the end of 1996, Kathy Bail addressed The Sydney Institute. She is the editor of *HQ* magazine, former editor of *Rolling Stone,* and has also edited *Do It Yourself Feminism,* a collection of essays by young feminists.

Bail had nothing to say about an Australia in which people left the front doors of their homes unlocked, nor did she raise the question of whether people were living in contentment and harmony with their fellow human beings. But her themes were as central and crucial for her as the themes in John Murphy's letter were for him. Bail was reiterating three basic feminist beliefs: that women should not be discriminated against on the basis of their gender; that women should earn equal pay; and that women should have the right to control their fertility. She offered her audience a caricature of a 'do it yourself feminist':

She always has the right line when a bloke at work makes a sexist comment; she has a modem (that she uses to access information and to network); she knows how to fix the spin cycle on a washing machine; she keeps a vibrator by the bed, she plays guitar, she likes wearing chest graffiti (a cheeky T-shirt that says something like 'Love Interest'), she was told that she could be whatever she wanted to be when she grew up (even an astronaut), she is obsessed with Barbie dolls, she draws comic strips, she always has an opinion on Melrose Place, she worships Lisa Simpson, she is particular about the colour of her lipstick, she believes action – from the bedroom to the boardroom – is everything, she feels that it's quite a good time in history to be a girl. She is full of contradictions.[2]

Kathy Bail concluded her presentation by quoting the words of 24-year-old Julie Martin, a fan of death metal music, from an interview published in *Rolling Stone*:

It is a very guy thing. Not many girls go to gigs. Maybe because it's just not very glamorous. Guys don't usually say anything to put you down but during a mosh, or something, they'll feel your tits and your bum. Well, they used to. We all fight back now.[3]

What might John Murphy and Julie Martin or, indeed, Kathy Bail, have to say to each other? Would it seem to them that they were living on different planets? Or would they simply attribute their differences – different interests, different values, different idioms – to the fact that they are members of two different generations that happen to lie at almost opposite ends of the age spectrum?

In between those two generations are the Boomers, a generation often criticised by their parents for having failed to maintain the values they were taught; often criticised by their children for saying one thing and doing another. (What generation of parents were not criticised for that?) Boomers don't need their parents or children to criticise them, though; they are self-critical enough. In *Fear of Fifty*, Erica Jong captured the mood of many Australian Boomers:

My generation is strewn with divorces. Looking back, we often wonder why. What did we gain by *not* staying together for the sake of the children? Did we gain anything at all?

We were the generation that was going to live forever. And we've turned 50 like everyone else. We're not going to beat the *malach ha-movis* [Angel of Death] after all.

Sometimes it seems both our kids and our parents were smarter than we were. We fell somewhere between our parents' Thirties idealism and our kids' Eighties cynicism. Somewhere deep down we still believe that *all we need is love, love, love.* Somewhere deep down we question how we got grey hair. How on earth did we get to be the grown-ups?

The wonder is that our kids are growing up – despite all that we did to destroy them.[4]

THE MEANINGS OF DIVERSITY

In Australia, we are accustomed to the idea of diversity. We are beginning to take some pride in the fact that our nation is being fashioned from diverse groups of both immigrant and indigenous people. (Immigrants have come here from 200 countries, and the Aborigines identify at least 260 nations as having coexisted here before European settlement.) We enjoy thinking of ourselves as cosmopolitan and in spite of some lingering uneasiness about the long-term implications of 'multiculturalism', we are willing to concede that ethnic diversity has become a significant thread in the pattern of our social fabric.

(In our two major cities, about 25 per cent of the population speak a language other than English at home, and seven or eight pages of the phone book are devoted to the name Nguyen. Such facts evoke both nervousness and pride, and either response is capable of being reinforced by politicians or cultural leaders. We can quite easily find ourselves drawn into downhearted resentment about the fragmentation of Australia's cultural identity, or buoyed by optimism about the inherent strength of an ethnically and culturally diverse society.)

Our awareness of ethnic diversity is accompanied by a growing sense of socio-economic diversity as well. Most Australians still think of themselves as middle class, because most contemporary Australians have grown up during a period when egalitarianism has been an important feature of our cultural idealism. The middle-class *mentality* remains strong, even in the face of economic evidence suggesting that there is a growing wealth class and a growing underclass (or a welfare-dependent class) which is collecting people who slip out of the traditional economic comfort of the middle class. (A 1997 report from the Centre for Population and Urban Research at Monash University showed that 32 per cent of Australian adults now depend primarily on welfare payments of various kinds, and 41 per cent of children under 15 years of age live in welfare-dependent households.)

Economic stratification has not yet become social stratification of a traditional kind, and it might never come to that, but the seeds of a new class structure have been sown and present economic trends, if maintained, would ultimately tend to erode not only the reality but even our perception of ourselves as being a middle-class society.

Whether we explore economic, ethnic, social or cultural dimensions, it is becoming harder to talk with confidence about mainstream attitudes and to describe the typical Australian or the typical Australian way of life. In the past 25 years, we have been so busily reshaping our society that many of our previous assumptions have been overtaken by events. What is a typical Australian family? Although about 80 per cent of dependent children live with both their natural parents, almost one million live with only one parent: that's too big a group to leave out of any discussion of the mainstream, to say nothing of the blended families, step-families and families based on *de facto* marriages which are becoming increasingly apparent in the Australian social landscape.

We can still say that Australians, typically, marry once and stay married, but the minorities who never marry or who marry and divorce are becoming so large that, taken together, they almost equal the married-once-and-stay-married group. To exclude them from any attempt to construct a picture of 'typical Australians' would be both misleading and absurd. (We can say, too, that Australian babies are 'typically' born to married parents, but more than 25 per cent of them are not.)

Even when it comes to patterns of work in contemporary Australian society, it makes less sense to talk about typicality than about diversity. Well over one million Australians are either unemployed or under-employed, while those in full-time work are now working such long hours that their overtime, alone, accounts for another 500 000 full-time jobs. So the workforce in Australia is characterised by imbalance and inequity. The rapid rise in part-time and casual work further fragments the picture, with more than 25 per cent of paid workers in Australia now having part-time jobs.

When we try to define attitudes towards the prospect of Australia becoming a republic, or the current state of the gender revolution, or responses to our growing awareness of the degradation of our physical environment, the same kind of diversity can be found. Even when we describe Australia as a 'Christian country' (reflecting the way 69 per cent of the population describe themselves on a census form), this masks some intriguing complexity: church attendance has plummeted to an all-time low, there are more than twice as many Muslims as Jews living in Australia, and our fastest-growing religion is Buddhism.

GENERATION GAPS

In the midst of all this, it is easy to see diversity as a rather chaotic aspect of Australian life, and to overlook what might be one of the most significant of all its sources: the differences between three generations which are culturally dominant in contemporary Australian society: the Boomers, their parents, and their children.

Conventional wisdom says there will always be significant cultural gaps between older and younger generations, possibly arising from a natural tendency towards conservatism with advancing years, and an equally natural tendency towards iconoclasm and innovation in adolescence and young adulthood. Some perceived generational differences, though, are more a matter of stereotype than reality; the *Encyclopedia of Psychology* identifies some of the standard prejudices:

Young people consider their elders to be obstinate, obstructive and outmoded, while they themselves are accused by their elders of showing an inadequate sense of responsibility, lack of experience and idleness, i.e. they are not recognised as adults.[5]

But the people whose voices are heard in this book do not seem merely to be trading in conventional stereotypes. The generations born in the 1920s, the late-1940s/early 1950s, and the 1970s could arguably be described as the products of three quite different Australian societies.

The older generation are the children of the Great Depression and the adolescents and young adults of World War II. The middle generation are the classic postwar Boomers who grew up in a period of unprecedented economic growth and prosperity, overshadowed by the menace of the Cold War. The younger generation have been born into a society experiencing such radical and relentless social, cultural, economic and technological change that it is fair to describe it as a society in the process of reinventing itself.

The differences between these three generations, therefore, are likely to reflect far more than their relative positions in the life cycle: those conventional generational differences are compounded and overlaid by the fact that these three generations symbolise three different eras in 20th-century Australia.

It is no surprise that the term 'generation gap' entered common parlance in the 1960s to describe the emerging social and cultural differences between Boomers and their parents. The nature and extent of those differences seemed so surprising because they were actually symbolising a profound culture shift in Australian life. Now the Boomers are themselves parents and are discovering to their alarm that the gulf between them and their parents is being matched, or even exceeded, by a culture-gap between them and their own children. As the rate of social change continues to accelerate (particularly under the influence of the Information Revolution), the rising generation will inevitably face a generation gap of their own (which perhaps will not only be between them and their children, but also between them and the generation right on their heels).

11

No wonder the Boomers so frequently describe themselves as feeling 'caught in the middle', as though they are the jam in some kind of cultural sandwich. They are possibly the first generation in Australian history to feel that when they look at both their parents and their children, they see generations with world-views quite different from their own.

The creation of a cohesive and harmonious society depends on our willingness to understand each other's points of view and, in particular, to recognise that each of us is the product not only of our unique genetic inheritance, but also of the social and cultural influences that shaped our early lives.

It is easy enough to comprehend that point, and even to put it into practice through the exercise of tolerance, when we are confronted by ethnic diversity: we can readily appreciate that someone whose childhood was spent in Greece, Vietnam or India is likely to have acquired a different set of attitudes and values, and a different outlook on life, from a person whose childhood was spent in suburban Australia. We can even acknowledge that a person raised in rural Australia is likely to have a different outlook from a person of the same age raised in the city.

But we are not always so ready to acknowledge that in Australia at the end of the 20th century, the differences between today's grandparents, parents and young adults are, in many ways, just like ethnic differences. (In some cases, of course, they are ethnic *as well as* generational differences: many children of postwar immigrants report a particular difficulty arising from their parents' determination to impose the inflexible values and standards from 'back home', not realising, perhaps, that things might also have changed 'back home'.)

Boomers, their parents and their children are living together in a rapidly evolving society which only seems 'normal' to the youngest of the three generations. Older Australians might cling to the idea that if only their values were more widely adopted, life would return to 'normal'. Sooner or later, though, all of us will have to acknowledge that the present situation, with all its ambiguities, uncertainties, contradictions and inconsistencies, *is* normal.

Social harmony and moral maturity depend on our ability to accommodate the gaps that have the potential to divide us – ethnically, culturally, intellectually, politically, economically, and generationally. If we are to bridge the generation gaps, in particular, we shall have to start listening to some of the things the three generations are saying about themselves and each other.

2
BORN IN THE 1920S: THE 'LUCKY' GENERATION

The *Lucky* Generation? A generation whose childhood and adolescence were darkened by the twin shadows of the Great Depression and World War II?

To subsequent generations of Australians, the children of the Depression might be seen as peculiarly *un*lucky. After all, the formative years of their lives were characterised by hardship and deprivation. They were growing up in a society where the rate of unemployment had exceeded 50 per cent. If their own fathers had work, then they were probably sharing food and clothing with their cousins, their neighbours, or other members of the community less fortunate than they were. Although they might typically recall their fathers with pride and respect, they might equally recall a certain aloofness in the relationship. Members of the Lucky Generation might have regarded their fathers either as desperately hard-working men who scarcely had time for a holiday, let alone for regular recreation with their children; or as rather embittered, disappointed men whose life potential was snatched from them by the tragedy of a worldwide depression at the very time when they were hoping to establish families and careers.

Some of them might recall a hero returning from the Great War, only to find that the society he fought for would treat him as ruthlessly and unsympathetically as it was treating everyone else. The children of the Depression were familiar with the sight of unemployed ex-soldiers begging in city streets; they heard dreadful tales of returning diggers who had been denied a pension; they knew that heroic service did not guarantee bread on the table.

In his book, *The Human Face of the Depression*, Michael Cannon recounts some famous examples of World War I veterans who fell on hard times in the Depression. In particular, he describes the fate of three Victoria Cross winners: William Joynt, who lost his dairy farm and was forced onto the dole; Albert Jacka, a Gallipoli hero who became a pauper, selling cakes of soap in Melbourne streets; and Hugo Throssell, whose real estate business collapsed and who eventually committed suicide in the face of unemployment and crippling debt. All three heroes, like tens of thousands of other men and women at the time, received no help or support from a government unable to relieve the suffering of its people.

Cannon estimates that, of the 450 000 industrial employees in Australia in 1929, almost one-quarter lost their jobs within 12 months. State banks collapsed and the number of business insolvencies more than doubled between 1929 and 1931.[1]

So it is not surprising that the generation born in the 1920s regard themselves as being luckier than their parents' generation. But this is not simply because, as adults, they were spared the challenges faced by their parents; it is partly because, as children, they had to endure the hardships of the Depression – hardships which, in retrospect, they see as having been a wonderful preparation for their subsequent, more comfortable existence. In fact, when the children of the Depression look back on those early years, they express gratitude for having had such a tough time of it, and often try to outdo each other with stories of just how deprived their childhoods were.

This is not to suggest that privation, of itself, is something to celebrate. In the case of the generation born in the 1920s, the luck they now acknowledge has more to do with the *timing* of each of the phases of their journey through the life cycle. In many ways, they see themselves as having been a 'charmed' generation: their lives began in hardship, then blossomed during one of the most extraordinary periods of economic and social development in Australia's history. In their own view, this generation got their timing right quite by accident: they believe that the lessons they learned in the Depression were the best possible preparation for the undreamed-of prosperity and comfort which their middle years would bring. In childhood and adolescence, they constructed a framework of values which would allow them to keep their heads when the attractions of material prosperity beckoned:

> *I'm lucky. I've always had a theory, based on my own lifetime, that I was born into the peak possible time and place in history. My parents did it tough in the Depression, but that taught me some of the most important lessons of my life. Then I was too young to fight in World War II, but I got the benefit of the revolution that was going on in education. By the time I was ready to look for a job, employment was easy. I was able to afford to buy a house and lead a far more comfortable life than my parents could ever have imagined. I feel as if I have lived like a king in the world – a nice little three-bedroom cottage with a garden, and a feeling of security which my parents never had. Such times might never come again: my own children are having a much tougher time than I had, and I hate to think what my grandchildren will have to face. Someone said to me the other day, 'Your world has gone, and it's not going to come back, but I'm sure you've been through the best.' And I think I have. We were poor in the beginning, but we were happy. We worked hard, but we have something to show for it.*
>
> *Life was much tougher for my father than it has been for me. I never even had to think about losing my job. If I didn't like what I was doing, I could change it.*

Members of the Lucky Generation regard the transition from a tough childhood to the prosperity of their middle years as evidence of having been dealt a very favourable hand by fate. By contrast, they regard their own children, the Boomers, as having suffered from the fact that, for them, it all happened the wrong way around:

an easy beginning in the boom years of the 1950s and 1960s, followed by the stress and trauma of the 1970s, 1980s and 1990s (see Chapter 3).

Looking back, the generation born in the 1920s consider that they have been more fortunate than both their parents and their children: they are located at the intersection of their parents' dreams and their children's nostalgia. The dreams of their parents were, in most cases, never realised and the nostalgia of their children strikes them as a tragic reflection of a 'truth' which has been gradually dawning on them: 'When we were young, the future looked rosy. Today, the past looks rosy.'

THE VALUES LEARNED FROM A DEPRESSION CHILDHOOD

In the Lucky Generation's reflections on 'the lessons of childhood', five themes recur: loyalty, saving, the work ethic, the sense of mutual obligation, and patriotism.

Loyalty

Values were completely different when I was growing up. Today, it is all dog-eat-dog but, when times were really tough and there wasn't the social security there is now, people knew that they had to stick together.

We used to tell the other kids that we got a doll or a book, or something, for Christmas but we just made all those things up. We never got toys like that, but you said that kind of thing out of loyalty to your family. You knew the other kids would make fun of your parents if they thought your family couldn't afford Christmas presents. But perhaps they were making up similar stories ...

When members of the Lucky Generation criticise the 'moral deterioration' of contemporary Australian society, they are more likely to mention loyalty than any other factor. They are proud of

17

the loyalty which, generally speaking, kept their own marriages and families intact, and which characterised their relationships with employers, shopkeepers, churches and neighbourhood friends.

Saving

This is the generation who, having observed the crippling effect of debt, came to believe that saving is a virtue and debt a dangerous burden. Of course, it is also the generation who willingly embraced the mortgage as a way of dramatically increasing the rate of home ownership in the Australian community. But the view that 'you shouldn't buy something unless you have the money to pay for it' was strongly inculcated in them by their parents and, indeed, by the direct evidence of their own formative years.

The same lesson that taught the Lucky Generation to save also taught them the virtue of life insurance: one sure way of 'taking control of the future' was to pay regular insurance premiums, not only in anticipation of a final payout, but also as protection in case of premature death. Indeed, one of the many differences between the Lucky Generation and the Boomers who would follow them is that the older generation believed in their long-term future (and in the need to prepare for it as prudently as they could afford to), whereas their children's generation showed little interest in planning for a future which they half feared might be borne away from them on the wind of a nuclear blast.

The work ethic

Not surprisingly, the Lucky Generation embraced the so-called 'work ethic' with a vengeance. They had seen what unemployment could do either to their own fathers or to relatives, friends and neighbours. They saw, through the embittered eyes of their own parents, the force of the proposition that 'if you are given some work to do, you grab it with both hands'.

Living out the work ethic was easier for the Lucky Generation than it had been for their parents, however. At the very time when they were crossing the threshold of the labour market, unemployment had dropped almost to zero. Not only was the

Australian workforce easily absorbing its returned servicemen and women, but it was also managing the transfer of civilian employees from the war effort to peace-time employment with remarkable success. The historian Geoffrey Blainey has described the period after World War II as 'an economic miracle because it brought full employment after a lean era'.[2]

Blainey notes the widespread fear that there would be a short burst of high unemployment after World War II, as there had been after World War I. 'But,' he says, 'the services people took off their uniforms and instantly found work in shops, foundries, road gangs, offices, schools and almost every occupation.'

In 1946, the Australian Prime Minister, Ben Chifley, was able to boast: 'Over 500 000 men and women have been released from defence and other government occupations. Yet at no stage has there been any significant number of unemployed.'[3]

Many of the people who participated in that economic miracle had already experienced the hardship of unemployment. But the Lucky Generation were new to the workforce and these were heady days. They knew that plenty of work was available and if one job did not suit them, another would.

The sense of mutual obligation

Though their recollections may be somewhat rose-tinted by the passage of time, the children of the Depression, in their later years, recall that their childhood taught them the tough lessons of moral responsibility, service to the community, and the need to accept the idea of mutual obligation as the glue which held society together.

Indeed, when they look about them in the closing years of the century, they believe that a declining sense of mutual obligation is at the heart of many of Australia's contemporary ills. In their view, people who do not accept some moral responsibility for the welfare of others will slip easily into self-centredness, vandalism and moral decay. This generation's understanding of the principle of mutual obligation extends beyond mere loyalty to family, friends, employers or retailers. It embraces the idea that, for a community to function properly, the needs of strangers must be taken into account:

> When you grow up with beggars on every city street and you know that there are people in your own suburb without enough to eat, you soon learn that you have some obligation to these people. I'm afraid that all the years of prosperity have led many people to forget that important lesson. But anyone who grew up in the thirties couldn't avoid it: you knew that sacrifices had to be made for the common good, and you knew that, at any moment, yours could be the family in trouble.

For some members of the Lucky Generation, the evidence of moral degeneracy shows up most vividly in the diminishing attention paid to matters of simple etiquette:

> When I was a youngster, we automatically stood up for older people on the bus or tram. You can forget that these days. Everybody's into equality and manners have gone out the window – especially when it comes to special consideration for older people.
>
> You can tell whether a community is functioning properly or not by the respect people show towards each other – especially people who are total strangers to them.

This generation's sense of moral responsibility and mutual obligation was rooted not only in the experience of the Depression but also in religious dogma. Whether or not they experienced a deep sense of spirituality, the members of this generation were typically exposed to some religious education, and the broad principles of Christian morality were generally familiar to them.

Patriotism

Partly because of their awareness of the many returned servicemen and women in their parents' generation, and partly because of the impact of World War II on their adolescence and early adulthood, the Lucky Generation developed a strong sense of national pride. Their patriotic faith was rooted in their belief in the rightness of Australia's position in the world as an unquestioning ally of Great Britain (and then of America), and as a cultural extension of Europe. This was a generation growing up in the Eurocentric era of the White Australia policy; they felt a close sense of affinity with Europe's 'New World' view of Australia. The ancient European tradition which had anticipated a kind of antipodean utopia fed into an Australian consciousness – particularly in the years immediately following World War II – that this was a country laden with economic, social, cultural and intellectual potential.

The patriotism of this generation was not confined to Australia; for many of them, it was also an inherited patriotism focused on Mother England, since they were all born and raised as British subjects who did not acquire the *legal* status of 'Australian citizen' until the proclamation of the Australia Act of 1948. They had grown up thinking of themselves as colonial subjects of the British crown, and they were generally proud of it. Ties with Britain were regarded with affection rather than resentment.

The Union Jack was prominent in their patriotic landscape and many of the institutions which dominated Australian commercial, cultural and religious life were unambiguously British or 'colonial' in character. The largest religious denomination was Church of England – generally referred to as 'C of E' – and it was not until 1981 that it was renamed 'Anglican'. (In yet another shift in the Australian cultural landscape, the 1990s have seen the Anglicans eclipsed by the Catholics as the dominant religious group.)

The Lucky Generation remember everything from Christmas celebrations to the clothes worn by their fathers (suit, tie and hat – even to the beach) as echoes of the British way of life. Not surprisingly, most members of the Lucky Generation now find themselves strongly resistant to the republican push in Australia. They cheerfully acknowledge that their emotional connections with Britain are so strong that they would suffer a sense of quite personal loss if the final, symbolic link with the British monarchy were cut: 'It would seem such an affront to the Queen'.

But the patriotism fed by loyalty to Great Britain was certainly not the whole story: an Australian identity was being shaped by the experience of two world wars; the impact of World War II, in particular, was definitive in reinforcing a peculiarly Australian patriotism as well.

Over the past 30 years or so, the Lucky Generation have experienced a steadily darkening sense of disappointment at what they perceive as their own children's apparent rejection of those five dominant values.

They look at their Boomer offspring and see a generation for whom 'loyalty is a thing of the past' (revealed, most vividly, in the escalating rate of divorce); for whom debt has become the new virtue (as a passport to instant gratification); for whom the commitment to the work ethic has been dented by the savagery of unexpected periods of unemployment in their middle years; for whom a rather materialistic self-centredness appears to have replaced the concept of civic duty; and for whom 'patriotism' seems almost to have become a dirty word.

Of course, the children of the Depression do not report unalloyed virtue in the values and morals of their own parents' generation. They often point to the bigotry of their parents, and to a rather rigid, self-satisfied conservatism which characterised their parents' view of politics, religion and culture:

In my father's day, the Catholics and Protestants wouldn't even talk to each other. Even though they all went to Church every Sunday, it wasn't all sweetness and light, by any means. My father was the ocker type that has largely disappeared now. Even though he had his good points, there was a lot of ignorance and prejudice attached to that type of character. I think we have become far more tolerant.

I admire him and, in many ways, I might have preferred his simpler lifestyle. But he was a pretty prejudiced old bugger, really. I hope I have taken on board the best of his very strong views on morality, but I am not as hidebound as he was.

This generation might regard themselves as having been more enlightened than their parents were, yet they consistently credit their parents with having set high standards which formed the basis of that greater enlightenment. It is as though the Lucky Generation are grateful for having inherited a set of very clear-cut standards which they were then able to modify and adapt in the light of their own education and, subsequently, their experience of a more complex society.

For example, women who were children of the Depression might praise their mothers for being ingenious cooks, for teaching them how to 'make do' with the most basic ingredients, and for managing to feed a family with limited resources. Yet, they will typically regard those same mothers as having had an inadequate understanding of nutrition and will reflect ruefully on the fact that their mothers' meals were often stodgy, unimaginative, repetitive, and sometimes downright unhealthy.

Similarly, the Lucky Generation praise their parents for having been strict in the raising of children, yet they recall that the 'house rules' were often absurdly rigid and claim to have been more relaxed and 'reasonable' in the raising of their own offspring:

I was married at 37 and I lived at home with my parents until then. My father was very much head of the house and he set a curfew of one a. m., even when I was in my thirties. My kids say, 'You're exaggerating, Mum,' when I remind them of this.

I am grateful to my parents, though, for setting such strict standards. Even though I was more relaxed with my kids, I still felt that some standards should be observed. In some ways, I suppose the standards just become more relaxed as each new generation sets lower standards for their kids. Perhaps the wheel will turn!

23

Whether the subject is discipline, patriotism, work, nutrition or marriage, the Lucky Generation typically express gratitude to their parents for having 'made the rules clear', even if those rules subsequently appeared excessive. Looking back, this is a generation who acknowledges that their parents' lives were so much tougher than their own that a certain rigidity and grimness was almost inevitable. Their parents' standards might have seemed extreme, even at the time when they were being imposed, but the Lucky Generation took from this experience the lesson that *some* standards are important; that parents have the right to impose their standards on their children; that 'authority' is to be respected; that life is not meant to be easy (let alone 'fun'); that life should be lived according to certain established principles, and under the willing constraint of accepted standards of behaviour.

AFTER THE DEPRESSION, THE WAR . . .

Most of those born in the 1920s were too young to serve in the armed forces during World War II – though some of the oldest members of that generation certainly became involved – but all of them were old enough to know that a war was on, to have some appreciation of the gigantic dimensions of that tragedy and its implications for Australia, and to realise that Australia was, for the first time since European settlement, under the direct threat of invasion.

The experience of a wartime adolescence – like the experience of a Depression childhood – was profoundly influential in forming the character, values and outlook of this generation. As with the Depression, they grew accustomed to the idea of absent fathers, uncles, older brothers and sisters, and to struggling, worried mothers. Their food was rationed. Luxuries were denied them. Stories of mass destruction and military setbacks were daily fare.

Yet, characteristically, they look back on World War II as an important ingredient in the making of the Lucky Generation. Those who were too young for military service regard that as a stroke of luck in itself, and even those who did join the armed forces and lived to tell the tale are typically inclined to describe their wartime experiences as uniquely 'character building'. The dominant theme in discussion of the impact of the war is that it had a positive effect in building a strong community spirit, a clear sense of national identity (in which 'Britishness' loomed large) and pride in Australia's capacity to make a significant contribution to the Allies' campaign. Leaving aside the prospect of an immediate threat to our own shores, the sense of participating in a great struggle against totalitarianism and fascism was uplifting.

Among those who participated and survived, the war often seems, in retrospect, to have been a great leap forward in their lives:

> *The Second World War was the best thing that ever happened to me. It was a good war for me. Up until then, my outlook as a working-class kid was to get a factory job or, if I was really lucky, an office job. But the war opened the possibility of training and going to university. I took the path of school teaching, so I was translated by World War II from working class to middle class, and I've never had an economic concern of any kind.*

> *I joined the navy during the war, so I got good wages, plus the war loading. That meant my wife and I could have a six-week honeymoon on the Barrier Reef, and we never had to pay off a mortgage, or rent. We never had money worries like the young people today.*

> *I borrowed someone else's aeroplane to fly when I was twenty . . . it belonged to the air force. I would never have had that opportunity if it wasn't for the war.*

For some families, the war was a blessing of a different kind. Recollections of childhood in the Depression are peppered with stories of physical violence against children. Frustrated, embittered, and often uneducated fathers, in particular, seem to have routinely vented their rage in physical punishment of their children (and, sometimes, in physical abuse of their wives). When a father emotionally and economically crippled by the Depression went away to war, this was a double relief to his family: they escaped the beltings, and they received a regular pay cheque.

The greatest impact of the war on this rising generation of young Australians was personal rather than political: its most vivid lessons, for those too young for military service, were about sacrifice and loyalty in the family and the community, rather than on the battlefield. The values learned from the rigours of the Depression were reinforced by the privations and sacrifices of life in wartime Australia.

Now, 50 years later, it is not uncommon for members of the Lucky Generation to assert that what the young people of today need is 'a good war'. Perhaps they don't mean that literally (and what could 'a good war' possibly be?); but what they might mean is that, for them, World War II seemed to have a clarifying, unifying and strengthening effect on the community. By contrast, they see contemporary Australian society as lacking a clear set of common values, being increasingly fragmented (by greater ethnic diversity, by frightening gaps between rich and poor, by the isolating and dehumanising effects of technology) and as going 'soft'.

The Lucky Generation are not, of course, suggesting that a depression and a war created a bed of roses for their early growth and development. On the contrary, they see themselves as having had to suffer, to sacrifice and to struggle in those early years; they recognise that their childhood and adolescence occurred at difficult periods in Australia's history; they believe that they have had to work hard to achieve what they have.

But they also have a deep sense of gratitude at the timing of it all. It was their parents and older siblings who bore the real brunt of those demanding years: by the time they themselves were entering the workforce, falling in love, marrying in record numbers and creating the baby boom, the world had fundamentally altered. They found themselves blinking in the bright light of the most dramatic period of economic growth and development in Australia's history – a time of social, intellectual, and cultural excitement as well. Who among them could have guessed that they were about to step onto such a rapidly moving escalator of opportunity?

AFTER THE WAR, THE BOOM!

The boom years following the end of World War II involved much more than an economic miracle. Contrary to all predictions, Australia was not gripped by postwar unemployment: the pool of labour swollen by returning servicemen and women, and by the early waves of refugees – dubbed 'reffos' in the 1940s – was soon soaked up by the manufacturing boom, the housing and construction boom, the boom in national development projects like the Snowy Mountains Hydro-Electric Scheme, and, ultimately, by a mining boom as well.

The rationing of food and clothing ended in 1948 and the consumer market began to be transformed by everything from the return of chocolate to the arrival of the first ballpoint pens and transistor radios and the re-emergence of advertising on a large scale. The first Holden appeared in 1948, ushering in the age of the family car (en route to the two- and three-car family). Television, automatic washing machines, revolutionary synthetic fibres, and a host of new gadgets from the Hills Hoist to the Sunbeam Mixmaster were just around the corner. Interstate and international air travel was about to be revolutionised.

But it was not just a matter of economics: everything seemed new; anything was possible. The whole world was changing. Hitler's henchmen had been punished, the state of Israel was created, India was partitioned, Russia had erected its iron curtain, the 'sound barrier' was broken by new jet aircraft, and, back home in Mother England, Princess Elizabeth was marrying her Prince Philip. An Australian, Dr H. V. Evatt, was elected President of the United Nations.

Geoffrey Blainey, writing in the *Australian Magazine,* argues:

The end of the war spurred a belief that Australia could be reshaped. The phrase 'the new order' was almost the catchcry of the mid-Forties. How to make the nation a fit place for returning heroes was the theme of countless books and pamphlets. This burst of utopianism and plain enthusiasm was reflected in the swing to the Left in politics. Presbyterian and Methodist pulpits held many ministers who thought that maybe a semi-socialist paradise on earth was now attainable.[4]

That sense of 'plain enthusiasm' is strongly reflected in the recollections of members of the Lucky Generation. They remember the 1940s and early 1950s as a time of bracing optimism, a time when it really looked as though that utopian dream might come true. After the refugees had been settled, the veritable flood of willing immigrants who followed them from Europe (seduced by a ten-pound fare) fuelled that possibility: after all, weren't they coming here because they knew that Australia was the land of opportunity, the New World?

(Incidentally, it was this view of immigrants – largely shared by the immigrants themselves – that led to official and widespread use of the term 'New Australian', to convey the idea that we were all building a new society and that people from other societies – other cultures – were coming here because they wanted to be assimilated into that exciting process. No wonder members of the Lucky Generation are still having some trouble coming to terms with anti-assimilation attitudes, and, indeed, with the concept of multiculturalism. To them, migrants were part of the dream of the new Australia, a dream based on middle-class prosperity in a land whose culture was – and, in their view, should remain – essentially British.)

In Blainey's opinion, the 1940s was a peculiarly influential decade: 'For a nation to face extinction,' he says, 'is the loudest of all wake-up calls.' He believes that serious public debate flourished more in the 1940s than it does today:

The topics of communism versus individualism, the churches versus secularism, the so-called 'brave new world' versus the tired old world, were discussed more intensely, and absorbed the minds and emotions of a higher proportion of the people, than any comparable list of topics today.[5]

Blainey, born in 1930, speaks eloquently for the Lucky Generation, characterising the postwar years just as they remember them.

Their response to all this enthusiasm and optimism was to set new records for the rate of early marriage in Australia. For example, the percentage of 20 to 24-year-old women marrying rose from 31 per cent in 1933 to 49 per cent in 1947, and then to 59 per cent in 1954. (For men aged 25 to 29, a similar trend occurred: 44 per cent of them were married in 1933, rising to 64 per cent in 1954.) The period now described by some demographers as 'marriage madness' stimulated the demand for suburban housing on a new and vast scale and, of course, created the baby boom.

And what a boom it was! From a prewar birth rate of 17 per 1000 of population, the Lucky Generation procreated at an unprecedented rate: in 1946–47, the birth rate rose to 24 per 1000, remained high through the 1950s and only began to fall away in the early 1960s. It was almost as if some official in a mythical Department of Procreation, imbued by postwar enthusiasm, had made a public announcement: 'Okay,' the official might have said, 'you've got 15 years, so get stuck into it.' (Of course, there almost was such a proclamation: the slogan 'Populate or Perish' had great currency in postwar Australia, and it didn't just refer to the need for immigration: people were actively encouraged to expand their families, and were offered the cash reward of Child Endowment for doing so. In any case, effective contraception was still some years away, so a heightened marriage rate almost guaranteed a healthy birth rate.)

Ask a member of the Lucky Generation about those heady years, when the ideal of egalitarianism seemed to be coming true; when the middle class was riding the wave of economic growth; when full employment was taken for granted; when one income could easily keep a family fed, clothed and housed; when Australians seemed sure of themselves and their future. Watch them smile as they cast their minds back to the 1950s. The recollection is mainly pleasant; the stories of comfortable suburban living are mainly happy stories. Yes, there was drunkenness (stimulated by the six o'clock swill in hotels compelled to close at that hour); there was boredom for some women who couldn't find fulfilment in family life lived in what seemed to them to be a suburban desert (and who had little hope of divorce or any other escape into an independent or different life); there was widespread industrial unrest; there was a Cold War and the faint fear that the Korean War could escalate into something regional if not global; but, generationally speaking, these were golden years.

They were not to last, though their glow would remain with the Lucky Generation forever. Something called the 'generation gap' was approaching, and it would symbolise for the Lucky Generation, as nothing else could, some of the ways in which their world was about to change.

As their children grew to adolescence and adulthood, they were forced to acknowledge that the old rules no longer seemed to apply. They had approached the boom years as their own parents might have, with their parents' values and some, at least, of their parents' scepticism about the seductions of materialism. But their children were not handling it like that at all.

'DID WE DO TOO MUCH FOR OUR CHILDREN?'

The postwar boom had felt like a stroke of unbelievable luck to the children of the Depression as they hit the crucial years of early adulthood. How could this be happening to them? What had they done to deserve it? (The answer for some of them was that they had fought in a war, but for most of them the correct answer was: nothing.) Why were they so blessed, when it was their parents who had struggled so hard to get them to this point? They were destined to be better educated than their parents, better fed, better clothed, better housed; they were poised to receive all the benefits of belonging to a society on a steep upward curve of growth and development.

Looking back on lives lived in such fortunate synchronicity with social and economic change, the Lucky Generation mention two causes for sadness, or, at least, for a tinge of regret and a nagging doubt.

The regret is that their own parents, generally speaking, never really reaped rewards proportionate to their perseverance, their determination or their moral rectitude. They might have died with a sigh of satisfaction; they might have taken pleasure in seeing their sons and daughters launched into a bright new world; they might, if they lived long enough, have themselves enjoyed, in retirement, some of the material comforts of the 1960s and 1970s. But it was their offspring who won the real prize: the fortunate combination of flinty parenting in childhood and a world of comfort and prosperity in adulthood.

Of course, the Lucky Generation pride themselves on their *own* ability to deal with the hardships of the Depression and the war but they know that, in a sense, they were along for the ride: it was their parents who bore the brunt of it. So they are grateful, but also regretful that their parents did not live long enough to see how it all turned out.

Such sentimentality is all very well, but it has its limits. Parents of the Boomers might wish that *their* parents could have seen them now, in the relative prosperity of their retirement years, but they are not at all sure that their parents would approve of the job they have done in raising their own children. Indeed, they are not altogether sure they approve of it themselves, and that's the source of the nagging doubt: Did we do too much for our children? Did we try too hard to compensate for the hardships of our own childhoods? Did we let them fall for materialism, without trying hard enough to inculcate in them the other values we believed in (though we believed in materialism, as well)?

Older Australians at the end of the century are facing the poignant possibility that the brutally honest answer to all three questions just might be 'yes'. But that answer wouldn't come too easily or too quickly. After all, another dimension of their luck was that they were becoming parents at a time when parenting itself

31

was being studied more closely and taken more seriously than it had been in their own parents' day. This was the generation who had Dr Spock's *Baby and Child Care* on the bedside table.

Although they praise their own parents' loyalty, hard work and commitment, the Lucky Generation were convinced, for most of their adult lives, that they were better equipped to be good parents than their own parents had been. They took pride in the idea of having a *relationship* with their children (even though the Boomers would say it was *they* who really pioneered 'good parent' territory, and *they* who have worked so hard at fostering relationships with their children). Boomers would probably be amazed to hear their own parents talking about the high quality of their parent–child relationships, since it is a favourite Boomer claim that they 'broke the mould' in this as in so many other areas of marriage and family life.

Lucky Generation parents believe three main factors made them better parents than their own parents had been. First, their own parents, especially their fathers, had to work so hard to make a reasonable living that little time was available to spend with children. As the workload became easier through the boom years, it was correspondingly easier for parents to devote time to the business of parenting.

Second, rising standards of education and other cultural changes made parents rather less rigid and authoritarian in their attitudes to child-rearing, with a positive effect on the quality of relationships between parent and child. In particular, older people speak of the fear which often infected their relationships with their fathers, but laugh at the suggestion that their own children ever feared them. (Boomer fathers, by the way, make a similar comparison between themselves and *their* fathers!)

Third, changing attitudes towards childhood itself, and an increased emphasis on the welfare of children, meant that children were generally better treated after World War II than before it.

Men in the Lucky Generation speak with pride about the time they spent with their children, the affection they showed them and the interest they took in their development. To hear their children

– the Boomers – talk would make these claims sound like an exaggeration, but they reflect the dramatic changes in attitudes to parenting which occurred during the passage from one generation of parents to the next. (In any case, there are plenty of Boomers' offspring who now complain that they don't see enough of *their* parents, so the truth about parenting skills is bound to be as elusive as the truth of any claims we make about our impact on each other.)

I know that my children have always been much closer to us than we were to our own parents. Things seemed to free up in the fifties and sixties, somehow. You could talk more openly . . . my parents were rather aloof in many ways. Dad worked like a navvy and Mum saw her main job as being to support him. It wasn't that they didn't love us, but they just showed it in different ways at that time. We have been much more expressive with our children and much more involved in their lives. And we are far more involved with our grandchildren than my parents ever were . . . but that's by necessity as much as choice, because our daughter is working and someone has to be there for the kids.

Further emphasising their good fortune, Lucky Generation parents acknowledge that not only were they educated to be, by their lights, better parents than their own parents were, but they managed to squeeze their parenting in before the institution of marriage was destabilised. The upswing in divorce figures since the mid-1970s and the progressive deterioration of traditional, nuclear family life (which had often depended on a stay-at-home mother to act as its foundation) has created a contemporary context for parenting which they regard as a challenge they were glad not to have to meet. When it comes to parenting, as in so many other aspects of their lives, they think they were luckier than their parents *and* luckier than their children.

Members of the Lucky Generation sometimes take refuge from doubts about their possible overindulgence of their children by remarking that economic cycles and conditions can be a huge factor in determining styles of parenting. They acknowledge that their parents often faced too much hardship and were distracted by too many survival issues to have the time or energy left for vital family life. Conversely, they wonder whether their own children were brought up at a time of such sparkling and seductive prosperity that, even with the best of intentions, they might have been powerless to protect them from the impression that material goals were all-important.

In trying to assess the quality of their parenting – as judged by the values espoused by their children – they feel uneasy. For all the contemporary Boomer talk about 'relationships' and 'quality time', members of the Lucky Generation wonder whether materialism might have crowded out some of the more subtle moral and spiritual lessons they were hoping to teach their children (and which, in turn, they hoped their children would pass on to the grandchildren). Instead, they complain about a growing emphasis on acquisition and consumerism – on possession as the goal – rather than on the uses of material comfort to secure the integrity and happiness of the family.

While there is a great readiness among the Lucky Generation to criticise their offspring for having become overindulgent parents, they constantly return to that nagging doubt: did we overindulge our own? 'If we did,' they are inclined to say, 'it was for quite different reasons: we were raising our families in an unexpected boom-time and material prosperity was visited upon us. We didn't chase it; we were just caught up in the consumer revolution.' Today, they would argue, parents too often seem to be deliberately using material possessions as a means of compensating for under-parenting. It's a recurring theme: 'If they haven't got enough time or energy to spend with their kids, they try to make up for it by showering them with the latest joggers, or video games, or whatever.'

But there are plenty of members of the Lucky Generation who will admit that they, too, went overboard in indulging their children in the 1950s and 1960s – not as compensation for inadequate parenting, but as compensation for their own deprived childhoods:

We wanted to give them all the things we weren't able to have when we were growing up. Of course, going without never did us any harm – quite the reverse, actually – but it's funny how you always seem to want to do more for your children than your parents did for you.

The tension buried in such remarks is obvious: it is the tension arising from wanting to 'do the best for your kids' while knowing that a bit of deprivation can be a good foundation for developing a realistic, feet-on-the-ground attitude towards prosperity when it finally came along. By contrast, they see their own children, the Boomers, as having grown up at a time of such material ease that they were not well equipped either to keep materialism in its place or to cope with economic upheaval and insecurity when it hit them in their middle years:

We were much more prosperous than our parents were and I suppose that rubbed off on the kids. We placed a lot of emphasis on the need to save, because that was what we learned from our own parents, but our kids just saw us spending. The next generation has been called the 'Me Generation' and with justification. They had the backing of lucky people like us who were financially okay – compared with our own parents – so we were insulating them from the reality they would have to face. I know our kids took things for granted . . . we had a car and a TV and a washing machine . . . you didn't think about things like that. I don't think they grew up expecting anything different.

The remark that 'kids didn't grow up expecting anything different' is one of those truisms which nevertheless helps to explain the gap between any generation and the next: children *never* expect things to be different from the way they are.

Lucky Generation parents shouldn't have been surprised (though they were sometimes shocked) by the fact that their Boomer children began their adult lives – especially their marriages – with the expectation that they could enjoy the same standard of material comfort to which they had become accustomed. Their parents might have complained that 'we started married life with a copper and an ice chest: our kids wanted too much, too soon' but to Boomers such comments have the irrelevance of prehistory.

In any case, the Lucky Generation brought it on themselves: they were so dazzled by their new-found prosperity and so proud of their new acquisitions – TV sets, radiograms, washing machines, electric food mixers, wall-to-wall carpets – that, in effect, they paraded their material affluence without realising that they were setting an example of consumerist fervour for their children. They might have known that they had saved for the things they had bought, but their children were more interested in the things they had bought than in whether or not they had saved for them:

> *Debt has become a way of life for our kids. They rushed into everything, and worried about paying for it some other time. They don't have the saving ethic that we had. We accepted that you had to have a mortgage for the house, but basically we saved up for everything else. They seemed to accept that you can just take out a loan for everything. In some ways I admire them, but I think they are going to run into a brick wall of debt. (Of course, we had the benefit of inflation to kick us along . . . our kids don't have the same security of knowing that the value of a house is just going to keep going up.) Too much, too soon, is never a good idea. It's not just that they get themselves in debt so quickly, but they never really appreciate what they have: they have their honeymoons in exotic places like Fiji . . . we went to Katoomba and thought it was a big deal.*

The Lucky Generation take pride in their own prudence and restraint and they like to think that those characteristics made a significant contribution to their own handling of new-found prosperity, because they took it sensibly and steadily, rather than recklessly. Although they concede the luck of living in a time of dramatic economic growth, they want credit for having 'kept things in proportion'. Now they are worried that their children and grandchildren are aiming for the same material standards, without the steadying effect of non-material values to accompany them.

For some members of the Lucky Generation, though, the problem runs even deeper than that. Doubt about whether they might have taught their children the wrong economic lessons sometimes leads them into an even more shadowy concern: was our failure to pass on non-material values part of a larger failure to 'keep children in their place'?

Certainly, contemporary grandparents are often appalled by what they see as the rising level of assertiveness in their own grandchildren, and a corresponding decline in parental discipline. On reflection, they can see that their own rather permissive approach to child-rearing might have been the beginning of a trend towards overemphasising the role of children in the family. While proud of their parenting, there is still room for anxiety about whether they 'let the pendulum swing too far'.

Perhaps this is nothing more than a traditional tendency for older generations to be critical of the values and behaviour of younger generations. Yet the Lucky Generation are slow to blame young Australians themselves for some of the differences in values between them: they remark that the behaviour of today's young people is probably a *symptom* of some of the major changes which have been taking place in the character of Australian society (most particularly, changes which have reshaped the attitudes and values of today's parents).

While acknowledging that the tendency towards taking children's rights more seriously should be welcomed and encouraged, the Lucky Generation are now concerned that the children themselves might have been encouraged to be too conscious of their own rights and too sure of their own importance. As grandparents, they are disturbed by signs that contemporary parents seem to be bending over backwards for their children, and that the children themselves regard this as not only desirable but appropriate.

Sometimes the tendency to yield too easily to children's demands is attributed to the fact that so many mothers now have paid employment outside the home that they are compensating for their own guilty feelings at not being more available. Sometimes a simpler explanation is offered: that baby-boomer parents are so preoccupied with themselves and the complexities of their own lives that they have actually *neglected* their children, even while portraying themselves as being utterly child-centred. This rather more cynical view assumes that Boomers' protestations about 'putting the children first' are actually a smokescreen:

> *I wouldn't like to raise children these days, with all the pressure they're under. Look how much you have got to be at their beck and call and how much worse the peer pressure is. Parents don't seem to have the time to spend with their children, so the kids spend more time with each other and I think they make up their own rules. I've been working at the local school and the boys come through the gate swearing and talking rudely and I say, 'You're not talking to your parents now, boys.' When you watch teenagers with older people, you notice that there's been a change in control. Parents don't have as much control over what their children will do. We try to avoid travelling on the train with young people. There's no way they'll stand up for anyone – they just sit there and yell and scream . . .*

But the Lucky Generation don't have their heads in the sand; they know the world has changed; they are relieved not to be in the thick of child-rearing themselves. Even at school, they believe that the rising generation are being treated quite differently, in ways which contribute to the tendency to believe in their own importance:

> *The daughter of a friend of mine is teaching in secondary schools and she is having a lot of difficulty controlling the kids. They call her by her Christian name and they seem to have no respect for her. To be perfectly honest, I'd rather teach 120 kids when I was teaching than 30 kids today, because, my God, it's a hard 30.*

There's one other sign which suggests to Lucky Generation parents that they might have indulged their children a little more than they should have. As they watched the divorce rate rise among their children's generation, they found that they were being called on to provide care and support (and sometimes even accommodation) for their offspring, late into their own lives:

> When we left home to get married, our parents knew that was the last they would see of us – in a manner of speaking. Today, you might find your kids leaving home to live with someone and then coming back, or moving back home after a broken marriage. I remember when my daughter rang me up and said, 'Mum, you had better make up my room again . . . it's over.'

So the message from the Lucky Generation about parenting is clear: they are glad that they raised their families when they did, though they feel the burden of parenthood *and* grandparenthood falling more heavily on them than it ever appeared to fall on their own parents. Still, they appreciate not having had the economic hardship which their parents' generation had to contend with, and they are pleased not to be trying to hold a family together in the present unstable and potentially disruptive circumstances of a culture in transition. Once again, the word is *lucky*.

'ARE WE THE LAST GENERATION OF CARING WOMEN?'

There is yet another respect in which the generation born in the 1920s regard themselves as lucky: as young adults, they felt that they 'knew where they stood' on the subject of gender roles and responsibilities and they are generally pleased to have been able to stay one jump ahead of the gender revolution.

This is not to suggest that they don't regard the feminist cause as justified. Many of them – especially the women – are filled with admiration for the capacity of their own daughters to manage far more complex lives than they themselves were ever expected to lead. Many of them accept that the women's movement was long overdue and that the status of women in Australia has been immeasurably improved by the revolution taking place since the early 1970s. They certainly see the changing role of women as one of the most radical of the changes reshaping contemporary Australia.

But their response to the impact of the women's movement on the lives of their own daughters (and sons) is understandably complex, involving a combination of respect, envy, admiration, bewilderment, disapproval and anxiety. The dominant emotions are positive, but there is plenty of hesitancy as well. Recurring questions are:

- Why are our children's marriages so unstable?

- How did our family – with its long history of marital stability – become involved in divorce and its messy aftermath?

- How will our daughter ever find the resources to cope with the demands of her 'have-it-all' life (and why can't our son-in-law be more supportive)?

- Why should our son be expected to do so much more around the house when he has such a demanding job (and why can't our daughter-in-law be more supportive)?

- What will become of our grandchildren: aren't they the guinea pigs in this risky social experiment called 'women's liberation'?

- Why are we having to play such an active role as grandparents, just when we thought we might be able to slow down a bit?

Of course, there are grandparents in the Lucky Generation who are not asking such questions (or who have stopped asking them), because they have seen their daughters' lives blossom and their grandchildren thrive, even under the influence of what they see as the 'dreaded day care'. And there are women of this generation who dearly wish they had enjoyed the fruits of the women's movement in their own lives. (Of course, some did: some women born into the Lucky Generation were among the pioneers of feminism.)

But whether they are fearful or confident, admiring or critical, there is general agreement among women born in the 1920s that the lot of women in Australian society has changed irrevocably, for better *and* worse. Their reference point for assessing the changing role of women has been, of course, their own mothers. In *The Human Face of the Depression*, Michael Cannon describes some of those mothers thus:

> The almost forgotten heroes of the Depression were mothers struggling to preserve a facade of decency in areas devastated by unemployment. The accepted tradition in the world of the 1920s was that men went out to work while women stayed behind to care for home and children. The extreme circumstances of the Depression meant that many men had to range far afield to seek employment, sending back whatever money they could to their families, or sometimes never being seen again. Any of these circumstances placed a terrible burden on mothers, never sure whether they would have enough cash to pay the rent, or feed and clothe themselves and their children.[6]

Children who grew up in less straitened circumstances than Cannon describes nevertheless recall their great respect for their mothers' fortitude, resourcefulness and selfless adoption of the role of carer. Not surprisingly, when those children came to marriage, their model of the caring wife and mother was the one they automatically adopted. The prosperity of the postwar years meant that, generally speaking, it was possible for a middle-class family to live comfortably on one income, so the pattern of the breadwinning husband and the mother-as-housewife was reinforced.

This is the generation of women whose newly liberated daughters

41

would ultimately come to denigrate their mothers' role as 'doormat'. But to the mothers themselves, motherhood seemed – and still seems – special and precious. Indeed, many of the Lucky Generation of mothers suspect that their working-mother daughters are actually enslaved by their so-called liberation. They recognise that contemporary women have more financial independence which frees them to make more enlightened (and possibly more ruthless) judgements about the quality of their marriages, and to take the initiative in divorce proceedings without fear of financial ruin. But they wonder whether the price paid for such independence is sometimes too high – in stress, in insecurity, in reduced time available for mothering, and even in a more cynical approach to men and to marriage itself.

Even when they regard their daughters' marriages as happy and rock-solid, many of these women shake their heads in bewilderment at the effort their daughters have to put into paid work, just to make ends meet, to pay off a mortgage, or to raise the fees for their children's education at a private school. 'Our daughters think life was tough for us,' they say, 'but I wouldn't like to have to go through what she's going through. We were lucky, compared with her generation. She has no choice: she simply *has* to work.'

The revolution in gender roles and responsibilities, while seeming to have created far more choice for Boomer women, strikes many of their mothers as having imposed great pressure on them:

In my day, you left school at 15, went to work in one of the few jobs thought suitable for women, lived at home with your parents and waited for Mr Right. When you got married, you moved out of the family home, stopped work (especially if you were a teacher or worked in the public service, where they wouldn't employ married women), and began having babies. It was sort of like a tunnel, and you just kept moving through it. You didn't have many decisions to make, really, except for who you would marry, where you would live, and how many children you would have.

It's a different story today, though. Girls decide when they will leave school, and most of them stay right to the end of secondary. Then they decide whether to go on to tertiary education or get a job, and a lot of them are thinking 'career'. They decide when to leave home, whether to flat with someone, when to start having sex, whether or not to move in with the boyfriend, whether or not to have a baby, whether or not to get married, whether or not to stop work.

I suppose it's good, in many ways. They really are just as independent as the boys. But it's certainly a different approach, and, to be truthful, I'm quite glad I didn't have to go through all that. It was much simpler in my day, and I'm quite pleased with the way it all turned out. It wasn't a dream run, but it isn't for them, either. My marriage wasn't perfect, but I'm proud of having stuck to it. My daughter thinks I should have packed it in years ago, but where would I have gone? What would I have done? I suppose that's the point she keeps making: she's free to decide that kind of thing. But I don't regret what I did; not at all.

She's brought up her three children, alone, since the eldest was seven. She's maintained a home and worked full-time as a teacher. I don't think I could have done it. I really admire her, and I admire some of her friends in similar circumstances. A lot of them have taken the disadvantages they faced and turned them around, despite great difficulties. Life was easier for us, not having to work and to handle all the crises that arise without falling into a hole.

It would have been scary for me to have a paid job as well as looking after the house and the children. I don't think I could have done it, even if I had wanted to. And I certainly never wanted to: I would never have been keen on the idea of missing out on those precious years with the children. Even my own daughter admits that she used to like knowing I was always there for her. That's where my energies were directed and I didn't question the worthwhileness of it. Actually, compared with my own mother, I thought I was pretty independent. I had all those labour-saving machines my mother never had and, of course, the car. I could get in that car and go!

43

We thought our mothers had a dreadful life, being tied to the house so much and having to contend with so much drudgery. But now our daughters think we've had a dreadful life: mine thinks I was a doormat to her father. But I simply don't feel like that. Although I admire what she's achieved, I think my daughter is a bit of a doormat to her children and her job, so perhaps no generation gets it quite right.

It is typical of women in this generation to describe themselves as 'carers' or 'homemakers' and to take pride in such terms. Though they now recognise that the roles offered to them in the labour market might have been limited – as nurses, secretaries, teachers, factory workers – they insist that the satisfaction they were seeking in their lives was always going to come from devotion and commitment to the care of their families rather than from paid employment. For them, the nurturing role was pre-eminent and, even now, they are reluctant to concede that any alternative approach would have brought greater satisfaction.

The nurturing role was not confined to mothering. The focus of 'carers' included their husbands, and the way some Lucky Generation wives talk about their attitudes to their husbands would make their feminist daughters' hair stand on end:

It's up to you to look after your husband. After all, he's gone out and worked hard all these years, hasn't he? It's up to you to fit around him.

But such women were also conscious of their responsibilities in the community: school tuckshop duty was taken for granted, many took their place on the roster for arranging the church flowers or a shift in the volunteers' shop at a local hospital, and others helped in countless ways to raise money for all kinds of charities. For many of these women, attitudes towards community service were established early in life: they learned from their own mothers that the war created an inescapable responsibility to provide whatever support was needed. The Red Cross and Legacy were particularly significant in harnessing this sense of moral obligation. Because they did not, typically, have paid employment outside the home, the women of the Lucky Generation were ready, willing and able to undertake all kinds of voluntary work in the community (work for which, at century's end, it is becoming increasingly difficult to find volunteers).

All these years later, the general attitude of women who saw their lives in terms of care and service is that they were secure in the knowledge that they had done the right thing; that they had discharged their responsibilities as they understood them; that they were free of any guilt associated with the possible neglect of their children and, indeed, regarded the mark of their success as being the way their children turned out:

> *If you want to know whether we are happy, it all comes back to how we feel about our families – how our children have turned out. That's how we judge ourselves.*

Having devoted themselves so wholeheartedly to mothering, it is hardly surprising that Lucky Generation women are inclined to blame changed circumstances for some features of their children's lives of which they can't easily approve (high divorce rate, working mothers, reluctance to save and keenness to spend). Although there is that niggling doubt about the possibility of their postwar indulgence of their children, Lucky Generation mothers are still proud of the effort they put into mothering: if their children have 'lost their way', they say, then 'the world is a very different place from the one in which I raised my family'.

Almost without exception, women of this generation who gave up paid employment after the birth of their first child do not, even now, regret the decision to do so. They believe their mothering, their housekeeping, their voluntary work and the support they gave their husbands were appreciated and respected and it is only now, as they face the challenges thrown up by their own daughters, that they feel the need to defend themselves.

Their defence of their roles as 'non-working mothers' is often aggressive: they resent any suggestion that life could have held more for them and they believe that contemporary women, for all their enlightenment and all their new-found gratification in paid work, are running the risk of raising a generation of children who will suffer from a reduced level of active mothering.

Sometimes these women will extend their defence to the point of attacking 'working mothers' on the grounds that by taking jobs which might otherwise go to young people, they are contributing to the long-term problems of youth unemployment:

There wouldn't be nearly such an unemployment problem among school leavers if married women were not so determined to rush out to work and neglect their own children.

(Exquisite pleasure is taken in the finding of any examples – real or mythical – of mothers who are going out to work while their own children are unable to find a job.)

Occasionally, women of this generation will find themselves momentarily destabilised by arguments with their daughters over whether or not they had been mere doormats to their husbands and families. Although they might grudgingly admire the enterprise and independence of some younger women, they certainly don't envy the conflict of values, the emotional strain and the sheer physical fatigue which many working mothers appear to suffer. Ultimately, they are prepared to leave the defence of their own lifelong commitment to a caring and nurturing role in the home to what they regard as the empirical evidence: they expect that today's generation of children will not turn out to be as happy, well loved, cared-for and secure as their own children were. (In this, they are often supported by the doubts and anxieties of their Boomer daughters who, for all their enthusiasm for a more complex, flexible and liberated view of women's roles, ruefully wonder whether they are, in fact, falling short in the one area where their own mothers excelled.)

'We knew where we stood.' That assertion, frequently made by women in the Lucky Generation, expresses an important aspect of their self-esteem. They knew what their roles were, and they performed them to the best of their ability. They knew what it meant to be a wife and mother; they knew how women were expected to act; they knew what to expect of a man (and their expectations were generally lower, or more tightly focused, than their daughters'). While they acknowledge that the world has changed and that traditional distinctions between the roles and responsibilities of men and women are blurring, they also believe that greater complexity and flexibility in this area increases the potential for conflict, stress and breakdowns in relationships.

'SOCIETY SEEMS TO BE DETERIORATING'

Coming to century's end from a life characterised by feelings of optimism and security, the Lucky Generation are saddened by the contrast they find between past certainties and present uncertainties; between the sense of security which they enjoyed for most of their lives and the sense of insecurity which is beginning to rattle them.

That insecurity has several dimensions. The first, and most specific, is that older Australians have come to the reluctant conclusion that they are no longer as physically safe as they once were. Although they are in the age group least likely to be physically assaulted, they harbour a disproportionate fear of physical assault. They believe that they can no longer rely on the assumption that Australian cities, towns and suburbs are safe places in which to live and move about, especially after dark. They have accumulated enough direct or indirect evidence of burglaries, muggings, physical threat or assault of various kinds to have developed something of a fortress mentality.

The Lucky Generation complain that their freedom of mobility has been restricted by their fear of physical violence and, when they find themselves being more cautious – about going out, travelling alone, or getting home before dark – they express regret that 'society has come to this'. They have always believed that freedom is one of the core characteristics of Australian society: anxieties about physical safety are therefore particularly potent because they challenge that belief:

> *I'm glad I grew up when I did. When I was first married, we could leave the house open and go out and my wife used to leave her bicycle in the street and know it was safe. Not any more. These days, if you are working in the front yard, you have to lock the back door. I hate all this obsession with security, but you have to protect yourself.*

They also feel that their 'peace of mind' is under threat. The more they observe of change in contemporary Australian society, the more uneasy they feel. Many of them still experience feelings of serenity and contentment associated with retirement and old age, but such feelings are often tainted by sadness about 'the state of the world'.

Sometimes this is expressed simply as a general sense of pessimism about the future (in particular, about the uncertainty of employment for their children and grandchildren). But sometimes the feeling is more specific and intense than that: it amounts to growing doubt about the integrity of our society and an uneasy sense that the 'shared values' associated with Australia's past are no longer so easy to identify.

It is probably not going too far to say that the Lucky Generation believe that Australian society is in a state of deterioration: in spite of their admiration for many of the advances made in technology, education, the position of women and – of great relevance – in medical science, they believe that society is paying too high a price for the changes it is embracing. Part of their view of themselves as a 'charmed' generation is the belief that when they were approaching adulthood, society was entering a period of economic and social development which was obviously beneficial. Today that process appears to have accelerated to the point where the benefits are no longer so obvious.

In their capacity as our tribal elders, the Lucky Generation persistently refer to the twin problems of 'declining moral values' and 'a loss of the sense of belonging to a community'. In fact, these two problems are really just two aspects of one issue.

In making a connection between 'morality' and 'community', the Lucky Generation are tapping into ancient wisdom: they are acknowledging that the moral sense is essentially a social sense and that it is from the experience of living together in neighbourhoods and communities that we develop the sense of mutual obligation which is fundamental to any ethical framework:

All these things go together. When I was a young bloke, people in the district knew each other. You could go to the shops and they knew who your parents were, or if you got into a spot of bother, the local cop would clip you over the ear and send you home. Today, kids can run wild and no one knows who they are. People don't have the same kind of morality if they don't feel as if they are part of a community.

The Lucky Generation cite a number of 'symptoms' to support their argument that society is breaking down: the declining standard of TV programs, the slow death of local neighbourhood shopping centres, excessive permissiveness in the raising of children, rampant materialism, increasing violence, growing dependency on drugs and alcohol, a decline in the work ethic, and a reduced emphasis on the value of the family. These are regarded as symbols of a society that seems to have lost both its sense of direction and the values which have traditionally underpinned it.

Older Australians believe that one of the characteristics of contemporary society is that authority figures are not accorded the same degree of respect as they once were and that this general decline in respect for authority extends to the elderly as well. At a time when older people acknowledge that they are being better looked after than their parents' generation were (for example, through pensions and access to retirement housing), they nevertheless believe that they live in a society which places undue emphasis on youth and does not have any automatic respect for its older citizens.

They are reluctant to blame young people for this state of affairs: they believe that young people are the product of an overly affluent and overly permissive society in which a general lack of discipline, at home and at school, has produced the 'inevitable' consequences.

Some members of the Lucky Generation speculate that one of the factors contributing to a declining respect for authority in contemporary Australia is the behaviour of people at the top, politicians and the judiciary in particular. Bad parliamentary behaviour and 'light sentencing' are two factors which cause feelings of despair among older Australians. While they believe that their parents' generation might have been too strict, too rigid, too moralistic and too proper, they nevertheless believe that the pendulum has swung too far in the other direction and that, in our attempt to be a tolerant and flexible society, we may have hastened the erosion of 'traditional values' and contributed to an overall decline in respect for those in authority:

> Society has certainly changed, but has it changed for the better? I don't think so. I think when people lose their sense of values, we are bound to get into trouble. Our parents might have had a tougher life, but our children are having more worries, more stress and more anxiety. Better values lead to a better life.

Perhaps paradoxically, the Lucky Generation have noted the rise of political correctness with great disdain. They are aware of the pressure on them to be more careful in their speech – particularly in the elimination of sexist and racist language – and they see this as yet another loss of freedom. Having to think carefully before you speak, 'in case someone takes it the wrong way', is regarded as a particular irony by older Australians who feel that, in most respects, members of contemporary society are becoming more careless of convention and less respectful of each other.

Looking back, the Lucky Generation see their lives in terms of a steady progression in the direction of realistic goals. They believe it is harder for families to plan confidently today because, in so many ways, they see society as being unstable and unpredictable. If this is 'progress', they argue, it is a very different kind of progress from the evolutionary, straight-line development which they recall. Such judgments are undoubtedly tinged by nostalgia, but the Lucky Generation do believe that contemporary Australian society, for all its sophistication and cultural development, is breaking down into subgroups (whether economic, ethnic or cultural) which threaten the relative homogeneity they seem to recall from the past:

> *Australia is not the kind of society I grew up in. Sure, there were a lot of poor people in the Depression, but we all pulled together. Today, the gap between rich and poor seems to be wider and we are not doing anything to close it. And there are a lot of other gaps as well . . .*

THE THREE BIGGEST CHANGES: TV, CARS, AND KIDS LIVING TOGETHER

When the Lucky Generation reflect on the many changes which have taken place in society during the span of their lives, they are astonished. They have lived through a world war and a Cold War. They have seen a society transformed by postwar immigration. They have seen the advent of jet flight, space travel and, now, the promise of virtual reality. They have watched the telephone shift from novelty to necessity and the family car become commonplace. They have seen the mass media transformed by television and, most recently, by the Internet, and they have seen their beloved wireless itself transformed by a shifting media context. They raised the first generation of children for whom 'popular music' meant rock-and-roll. They witnessed the sexual revolution, the rise of Women's Lib, the emergence of a drug culture, and the social consequences of all these upheavals, including the consequences for their own families. They have seen Mothers' Day and Christmas become uncompromisingly commercial. They have witnessed the waxing and waning of fashions in primary and secondary education, and the dramatic expansion of tertiary education.

As a generation, they regard themselves as having been largely untarnished by many of these changes. Because their parents encouraged them to make a commitment to security and stability, they believe that they have reached their retirement years with that commitment largely intact.

In discussing the social and cultural changes they have witnessed, the Lucky Generation identify three as being particularly symbolic: television, car ownership, and young couples living together before marriage.

Television

Television entered the lives of this generation when they were aged between their late twenties and late thirties. By then, they had generally completed their education and their courtship. They were often already raising a young family when they bought their first TV set. At the time, TV was undoubtedly the most radical technological innovation in their lives and, all these years later, its symbolism is so powerful for them that they still identify it as a dramatic reshaper of our society.

For this generation, TV arrived in a blaze of almost mystical enthusiasm. They assumed it would revolutionise their lives, offering information and entertainment in a previously undreamed-of fashion.

In the event, TV has been a continuous source of pleasure as well as a continuous source of disappointment. It has never quite lived up to its early promise and yet it has absorbed countless hours of the Lucky Generation's time. It is still special, almost magical, to them. They feel more affectionate towards TV and more aware of its *potential* value, even now, than younger people, because they still remember the miracle of its arrival. They complain that it has let them down, that it has robbed them of too much time, or that it serves up 'too much rubbish'. But they remain loyal to it and still tend to set aside formal periods for watching TV in a way which today's children find quaint. The Lucky Generation still find TV hard to ignore.

TV was a dominant feature of the childhood and adolescence of baby-boomer children, and the Lucky Generation express gratitude to the medium for the way in which it appeared to accelerate the learning processes of their children. ('They seemed to learn so much at a younger age than we did,' they say.) At the same time, they wonder whether TV was a significant factor in smothering the values they were trying to inculcate in their children; whether TV made their children too worldly-wise at too young an age; whether it gave their children access to too much 'easy' entertainment and stifled their ability to 'make their own fun'.

Contemporary TV is often criticised by this generation, as it is by younger generations, for its levels of violence, for its 'mindlessness', for 'pushing the seamy side of life at you', and for focusing on the sensational and the bizarre. And yet, many members of the Lucky Generation remain grateful to the medium and believe that it has indeed been something of a window on the world for them, because that is precisely what they expected it to be.

Today, of course, TV's significance to the Lucky Generation goes beyond its capacity to inform or entertain: it has become a symbol of the new age of information technology. No other medium will ever seem to the Lucky Generation to have been such a spectacularly innovative piece of technology as television; even the personal computer, for all its seductive (though often, to this generation, impenetrable) appeal, tends to be seen as a 'derivation' from the television screen. The difference between television and the mass media that preceded it – radio, newspapers and magazines – is unmatched, in their eyes, by the difference between TV and any of the media that have followed it.

Widespread car ownership

When the Lucky Generation was growing up, cars were a rarity, generally owned by the wealthy or the eccentric. Indeed, a car travelling down the street in the Depression was itself an object of special attention.

At the very time when the Lucky Generation came to adulthood and began establishing families, the Australian car industry entered a new phase. With the local production of the Holden, and the move towards virtually universal car ownership, an unprecedented level of individual mobility had arrived.

The Lucky Generation have willingly embraced the increasing dominance of their lives – and the places where they live – by the motor car, and they regard this as perhaps the single most significant symptom of the increased affluence and materialism of our time:

> *All these cars! That's one of the most significant ways in which life has changed. We all take them for granted now, and our lives revolve around the fact that you can always jump in a car and go wherever you want.*

For the women of the Lucky Generation in particular, access to the private car is regarded as one of the transforming differences between their way of life and the way of life of their mothers.

As with television, the significance of the motor car is not confined to the role and function of the car itself. The private car has become symbolic of a general shift from public to private space; of the rise of the individual; and of the extraordinary emphasis which has been placed on travel in the last quarter of the 20th century:

> *I wonder why everyone is in such a hurry to be somewhere else. At any hour of the day or night, the roads are full of cars. And you go to the airport, and there are all these queues and all these planes taking off and landing . . . people seem to have become obsessed with the idea that they must keep moving.*
>
> *The car is a great blessing, of course. It is so convenient and it has been wonderful for me. But I think that, as a society, we have gone overboard for the car . . . look how many people we have killed and how much we have polluted our cities by our desire to own so many cars.*

'Kids living together'
To their own amazement, the Lucky Generation find that they have come to accept the widespread practice of young people living together before marriage (though they are still struck by it to a

sufficient extent to remark upon their own acceptance of it). Many of them report the shock and disapproval which they felt when they first came upon people in their own family – perhaps even including their own offspring – who were determined to cohabit with a sexual partner before marriage. Robust arguments and even hysterical family fights are now recalled with some rueful acknowledgement of the fact that 'these things are common practice today'.

Although the Lucky Generation are proud of their own more solemn approach to marriage – and they sometimes express relief that their courtship and marriage took place before the excesses of the sexual revolution – they are also proud of the fact that they have been able to develop a generally tolerant attitude towards sexual liberation among their own children and grandchildren.

This is not to suggest that they entirely approve of all aspects of sexual liberation or, indeed, of the consequences of a more relaxed approach to sexual relationships. They express strong disapproval of sexual behaviour which threatens the stability of marriages, and yet they do regard the concept of 'trial marriage' among the young as a change which is probably for the better, 'as long as they are serious about it and not just sleeping around'.

The Lucky Generation sound a rather predictable warning: they might have come to accept the idea of 'kids living together' but they are critical of the concept of instant gratification and the thought that something as fragile and precious as marriage could be expected to work out without a great deal of effort and discipline. They are therefore wary of the idea of young people moving in and out of live-in relationships without a sufficiently serious commitment having been made. While they are prepared to endorse the concept of trial marriage, they believe that it is only 'safe' when it is just that: a trial period of something which resembles the commitment of marriage. 'You don't get anything – including a successful marriage – without working for it' is typical of the way in which the Lucky Generation apply traditional values to the most contemporary of phenomena.

A LUCKY COUNTRY ... FOR A WHILE

Listening to the Lucky Generation talking about their lives is a bit like consulting the tribal elders. They have accumulated vast experience; they've done most of the things they wanted to do, and many things which, in childhood, they would not have dreamed of being able to do; they have generally seen as much of the world as they have wanted to; they know about as much as they are ever going to know. They look back on 70-odd years of life with a curious sense of astonishment that it has all turned out so well for them: in spite of their fair share of personal tragedy, they know that as a generation, they have had the closest thing imaginable to a dream run.

Although they know they can't escape some responsibility for it, they have become highly critical of the state of the world. They believe that contemporary society is losing its way; that too many values have evaporated in the face of relentless materialism; that the rest of us will come to rue our own self-centredness; that the ideal of self-sacrifice is a thing of the past; that too many working mothers are neglecting their children and destabilising both family life and the labour market; that technology is clever but hardly likely to be our salvation; that instant gratification is a dangerous trap.

Ronald Conway, the Melbourne psychologist who was born in 1927, argues passionately that for his generation – growing up in the 'relatively safe, vehicle-free suburbs and towns of the Thirties' – the wretchedness of unemployment has tended to hide the loyal, no-nonsense, self-reliant way of life that such hard times can produce. Writing in the *Australian Magazine*, Conway raises a question which sounds as if it has come straight from the heart of his generation:

> Was this really the last of Australia's 'bed-rock' generations on which something distinctive and enduring could be built? The jury is still out, and the country has hardly yet found its soul.[7]

Another distinguished spokesman for this generation is Donald Horne, author of *The Lucky Country*. Having been born in 1921, part of Horne's great achievement in that book was to offer a critical analysis of the attitudes and values of the generation to which he himself belongs. When *The Lucky Country* was published in 1964, Horne's essential message was both provocative and alarming: he was warning his own generation that the boom years they had been experiencing were largely a product of good luck rather than good management or enlightened thinking, and he was alerting Australia to the potentially dire consequences that could flow from a continued reliance on luck:

> Australia is a lucky country run mainly by second-rate people who share its luck. It lives on other people's ideas, and, although its ordinary people are adaptable, most of its leaders (in all fields) so lack curiosity about the events that surround them that they are often taken by surprise. A nation more concerned with styles of life than with achievement has managed to achieve what may be the most evenly prosperous society in the world. It has done this in a social climate largely inimical to originality and the desire for excellence (except in sport) and in which there is less and less acclamation of hard work. According to the rules Australia has not deserved its good fortune.[8]

Beneficiaries of the welfare state

Looking back, it is hardly surprising that the generation born in the 1920s should have felt themselves to be peculiarly lucky. Rather than heeding Horne's warning, they – and their children – embraced the idea of 'the lucky country' as a rather charming and reassuring self-description. Australians of that era *liked* to think of themselves as lucky, and the expectations created by the boom years of the 1950s and 1960s led them to assume that their luck would not run out.

There's even some evidence to suggest that their luck *hasn't* run out. The very generation who benefited from low taxation when they were raising their families turn out to be the same generation

who now enjoy the provisions of a generous age pension. As the
New Zealand historian Dr David Thomson has remarked of the situation in his homeland: 'The 20th-century welfare state is looking
disturbingly like a one-generation benefit scheme'.[9]

In the tenth Bert Kelly Lecture (1993), the Perth philosopher
Alan Tapper analysed the idea of generational imbalance in the
welfare state, as it applies in Australia. Tapper noted:

> Net lifetime transfers to the generation which is now enjoying
> retirement have been massive. This generation benefited in the
> 1950s and 1960s, when the State favoured the young, and ben-
> efited again when the State later transferred its favours to the
> elderly . . . The lifetime personal income taxes paid by an aver-
> age couple from that generation will amount to only a fraction
> – probably less than half – of the value of the age pension they
> will receive.[10]

The dramatic increase in public funding of age pensions that
occurred in the 1970s (under the Whitlam government) and 1980s
(under Hawke) reversed the trend towards poverty for the elderly,
but it created a system which economic forecasters are now suggesting cannot be sustained. The taxes paid by the huge baby-boom
generation have funded the pension for their parents (as well as
unemployment benefits for their children), but who will fund the
pension for the Boomers when, in vast numbers, they reach retirement? Not their children, certainly, because there simply aren't
enough of them. (The Boomers' parents set the record for the highest birth rate this century; the Boomers themselves have set the
record for the lowest – though the Post-boomers may well drive it
even lower.)

3
POSTWAR BABY BOOMERS: THE 'STRESS' GENERATION

The phases of the Lucky Generation's journey through their life cycle – a tough start, then a dream run – could not have been more different from the experience of their children. For the Boomers, born during the years of unprecedented prosperity following World War II, it was all the other way around: a dream start, full of the promise of an endless prosperity, followed by turbulence and hardship in their middle years.

The baby boom was the outcome of two other booms which began in the late 1940s and lasted until the early 1960s: the marriage boom and the economic boom.

The dramatic rise in the postwar birth rate was a direct consequence of the rise in the rate of marriage. In *With This Ring*, Gordon Carmichael identifies 'early, almost universal marriage' as being characteristic of the 1950s and 1960s.[1] This was, in some ways, a response to postwar optimism. People were expressing their confidence in the future by marrying in unprecedentedly large numbers and, in turn, producing the babies that would create the baby boom.

The baby-boom generation itself, therefore, stands as a symbol of that optimism: such large-scale production of babies signalled a return to peace, normality and the contentment of stable family life. 'Home and family' became the focal point of an Australian society that was settling down to the serious business of middle-class, sub-urban prosperity.

And what prosperity it was! If the marriage boom was the demographic antecedent of the baby boom, then the economic boom was its cultural cradle.

Looking back, it is easy to say that Australians in the 1950s were less well-off than they are today: in the 1960s, a return airfare to London cost 21 weeks' average earnings; today, it costs about three weeks' earnings. The cost of a refrigerator is down from 10 weeks' earnings to less than two and the number of cars per person has increased by 75 per cent since the 1960s.[2] In terms of domestic appliances, gadgets and, in particular, telecommunications equipment, Australia in the 1990s appears far more prosperous than it did 30 or 40 years ago.

However, in terms of gross national product, Australia in 1966 rated seventh among the industrialised countries of the world, but had fallen to 21st on that scale by 1996. *Relatively speaking*, there-fore, Australia had a stronger economy then than now.

But the economic performance of Australia relative to other countries is not the main point: it was the Lucky Generation's *sense* of astonishing prosperity – and the related expectation of perma-nent economic growth – that dominated the culture in which the Boomers were growing up. The construction boom, the manufac-turing boom and, later, the mining boom all contributed to the feel-ing that Australia was economically invincible and that prosperity, symbolised by material comfort and a burgeoning middle class, was the birthright of the Boomers.

Unemployment was scarcely spoken of; indeed, there was so much work to be done that Australia was trying to attract as many immigrants as it could to swell the workforce. This was a time when Australians believed that the economic escalator would carry them infinitely upwards. No wonder the Boomers came to feel opti-mistic about the future and carefree in their approach to it. They knew they could get work whenever they wanted it, and they knew that it was possible for one income to sustain a conventional family in suburban comfort. They knew that this was the land of opportunity and that the future was rosy.

But the promise of endless prosperity was only half the story. The Boomers were actually being shaped by a most peculiar paradox: they were not only the children of the boom; they were also the children of the Cold War.

The Cold War was not just another 'phoney war', presaging a conventional military conflict. Its uniqueness lay both in the presence of vast quantities of nuclear weapons, with steadily increasing stockpiles on both sides, and also in the sense that this was a titanic struggle between communism and capitalism – two ideologies competing for world domination.

(In Australia, antagonism towards communism even led to a referendum proposal to outlaw the Communist Party of Australia. The referendum question was defeated, but the lingering belief that communism was essentially evil persisted even up to 1996, when a controversy broke out concerning pro-communist views of the historian Manning Clark.)

Spending their formative years in a world gripped by this struggle, the Boomers' world-view was inevitably influenced not only by a kind of Armageddon mentality, but also by the seductions of nihilism and hedonism characteristic of a society facing the possibility of extinction.

The Cold War spawned an entire genre of 'despair-and-deception' books and films based on the murky world of espionage populated by the devoted slaves of one ideology or the other. This was a dark period of moral ambiguity, fictionalised in such work as John Le Carre's *The Spy Who Came In From The Cold* and Len Deighton's *The Ipcress File* (and, with a lighter touch, in Ian Fleming's slick and sexy James Bond, and the TV spoof series, 'Get Smart'). The recurring theme in this genre was that, since the struggle was ideological rather than merely political or territorial, none of the conventional rules applied. The moral supremacy of 'our' ideology overwhelmed all other moral niceties. And underneath it all was the lurking sense of nuclear annihilation as the potential end-point of the struggle.

All the rosy expectations created for the Boomers by their economic circumstances were therefore tinged by a shadow: the ever-present threat of nuclear war. This was the period when the idea of

World War III was spoken of as though it was a kind of 'future historical' reality. The Boomers, as children and adolescents, knew more than they might have wished to know about the nuclear arms race and they lived with the possibility that some Russian or American might push the hot button, deliberately or accidentally, and wipe out the species. Both the Korean War of the 1950s and the Vietnam War of the 1960s carried the potential to escalate into ultimate conflict between the two super powers – the USSR and the USA. Boomers were presented with almost daily evidence of the underlying tensions of the Cold War, and they knew that if any regional war erupted into a major conflict between the USSR and the USA, such a conflict would have the awesome potential to become a nuclear holocaust.

So here was a most extraordinary pair of contradictory beliefs: the belief in a rosy, easy future and the concurrent belief in the possibility of *no future at all*. To understand the development of Boomers' attitudes and values, therefore, it is necessary to keep that paradox in mind.

What would such contradictory tensions do to a generation formed by them? Perhaps hindsight supplies too simplistic an answer to that question, and yet there does seem to have been an inexorable logic about the fact that this would become a generation obsessed with the idea that 'we're not here for a long time, we're here for a good time'. This is the generation who have become famous for their need of instant gratification: the generation who believe that, whatever they want, they had better *have it now*. The Boomers' impatience to consume everything from material goods to education, sexual experience and travel has become their hallmark. (Though not quite as impatient to marry as their parents were, Boomers were still far more impatient for marriage as their children are turning out to be: 30 per cent of Boomer women were married by the time they were 20, compared with only five per cent of their daughters' generation who are married at that age.)

The peculiar combination of contradictory influences on the Boomers, perhaps inevitably, created what has become widely known as the Me Generation: a generation whose catchcries became 'Do your own thing' and 'Look after Number One'; a generation who were destined to become poor planners, unenthusiastic savers but voracious consumers.

Here are some of the things economic and social commentators have been saying about them:

> The Baby Boomers have been the shortest-term thinkers of probably any generation for over 100 years. We are the only country in the Asia-Pacific that doesn't have a long-term plan. And they are our worst savers on record [in terms of saving as a percentage of income].[3]
>
> Philip Ruthven, futurologist and Chairman of Ibis Business Information

> Baby Boomers have inflated expectations of property because they are the generation which inflated property prices.[4]
>
> Rob Keavney, Managing Director of Investor Security Group

> Baby Boomers are not keen on planning: most have saved little for their retirement, assuming their real estate will somehow take care of it.[5]
>
> Susan Oliver, a former director of The Commission for the Future

Arun Abey, Executive Chairman of IPAC Securities, describes Boomers' reluctance to save with charitable obliqueness:

> Baby Boomers have a very strong cash-flow need.[6]

Reg Bryson, Managing Director of The Campaign Palace advertising agency:

> They are the most affluent, independent, self-indulgent, discerning and biggest-spending group of people the world has seen. Boomers just want to have fun . . . and it is in short supply in the lives of today's Boomers. Middle-age has been a time

of duty, obligation and responsibility, and they miss the good times. They want them back . . . [7]

Bryson's analysis accurately reflects the dilemma in which many Boomers have been caught. Coming out of a period of comfort and prosperity, they have hit the turbulence of an age of discontinuity: that period since 1970 when Australian society has been destabilised by the rapid and escalating rate of social, cultural, economic and technological change. Their parents' generation had their values established before they hit the 'Easy Street' of the 1950s. But the Boomers had Easy Street as their cultural cradle: it gave them a start which resulted in the lack of a clear moral framework and of a solid value-system comparable with their parents'. The things their parents said about values, religion and morality tended to be over-whelmed by the seductive evidence of a relentlessly materialistic society.

So the Boomers were ill-equipped for what was to happen to them in the early and middle years of their adult lives. In their quest for the personal happiness they had been led to expect, they have become our most-divorced generation. In their quest to maintain a high standard of material comfort, they have created the two-income household (and therefore the 'working mother') as the cultural norm. In the process, they have redefined the dynamics of family life.

They are the generation who were on the leading edge of the gender revolution, as Boomer women rebelled against the domestic ideal which had been presented to them by their married and settled mothers. They are also the generation who, having grown up with the ideal of egalitarianism rooted firmly in the prospect of universal economic prosperity, have been horrified to find society splitting into the haves and have-nots at such an alarming rate.

Many of the Boomers' dreams have turned sour. Many of their cherished hopes have failed to come to fruition. Their impatience to possess and consume has finally given way to an understanding that they are here for the long haul and the journey is going to be tougher than they expected it to be.

All of this has created a pervasive sense of *stress*. Indeed, it is fair to say that 'stress' has become the buzzword of the Boomers. It is almost as though they have adapted to their stress by becoming proud of it, wearing it like a badge of generational angst, or a medal for service in the combat zone of contemporary society.

Boomers' conversation is peppered with references to stress: even their typical greeting – 'How are you going? *Busy?*' – assumes that their friends will have been 'stressed out' by the pace and complexity of their lives. This is the first generation of Australians to have identified stress as a debilitating consequence of everyday life, and to have assumed that it is a key factor, perhaps even *the* key factor, in diseases and disorders ranging from heart attacks and cancer to marriage breakdown, 'road rage' and occupational burnout.

Boomers have become so preoccupied with stress that they are likely to attribute it to whatever circumstances they happen to find themselves in: the lonely burden of single parenthood, the complex demands of marriage, the strain of combining paid work with motherhood, the grind of being a full-time housewife, overwork, unemployment, or life itself.

ELASTIC ADOLESCENCE

Not surprisingly, the Boomers are now heavily into nostalgia. They are reluctant to part with their youth because they associate it with a time when everything looked rosier than it does today. They love to be reminded of the promise of their early years. They have become the generation who are still determined to stuff themselves into blue jeans in their late forties (partly to pretend that they are not as old as they are, partly to remind themselves of how they looked in their teens, and partly to symbolise their determination to 'stay close' to their own children). They are still playing the music of their youth and young adulthood; they still hanker after long hair; they are determined not to act their age. Volkswagen have even revived the Beetle car with the reported aim of cashing in on 1960s nostalgia among middle-aged Boomers.

Writing in *Business Review Weekly*, Neil Shoebridge and Adele Ferguson report that Boomer executives, rather than ageing gracefully, are fighting the ageing process:

> Worried about receding hairlines and expanding waistlines, they are joining gyms, buying exercise equipment, trekking over mountains and jumping into sports cars. Physical well-being is a popular topic among Boomers. (They no longer discuss health and fitness. As they get older and find strenuous exercise more difficult, they talk about 'well-being'.)[8]

Shoebridge and Ferguson quote a typical Boomer executive:

> 'I don't think there is much I can't do now that I couldn't do when I was 20.'

Boomers have invented the *elastic adolescence*, stretching all the way into middle age. This is turning out to be good news for the marketers of youth-oriented products and services who had feared that as the baby-boom generation aged, the market for their products would shrink. They needn't have worried; the Boomers are not about to retreat into cardigans and slippers. Having had the youth market invented for them, they intend to cling to it for as long as possible. Boomers, more than anyone, believe in the 'cult of youth'.

Quite apart from their desire to maintain a youthful appearance, Boomers have provided an unexpected commercial fillip in another way. Because their divorce rate has soared, many of them are re-entering the 'marriage market' for the second and third time, boosting demand for products and services traditionally associated with the rituals of courtship. Cosmetics, sports cars, hideaway holidays, sexy lingerie, candlelit dinners, weight-loss programs – all the paraphernalia of the sexual prowl is still being sought by the Boomers, even as their own children enter the romance market. Whether or not they are actually divorced and keeping an eye out for the next partner, Boomers know that marriage has become an inherently less stable institution than it was for their parents.

In this kind of climate, fed not only by the divorce rate but also by the sexual permissiveness of the 1960s and beyond, Boomers are likely to be more concerned about their attractiveness to the opposite sex than they believe would have been true for their parents. Even when securely married, the possibility of another potential partnering often lurks (sometimes hypothetically, sometimes comfortably, sometimes seductively).

The idea of romantic love being maintained or revived in their middle years is an appealing aspect of elastic adolescence. Their culture makes them open to the idea of intense sexuality and new ways of being sexy, even if they are sticking with the same partner. 'Marriage enrichment weekends' might be designed to improve the quality of personal relationships, but many of the Boomers who attend them are hoping for some kind of sexual renewal. (One factor encouraging Boomers to stay romantic – at least in their minds – is their belief that the 1960s was said to have been a decade of greater sexual permissiveness than their own personal experience seemed to suggest. For some restless and unfulfilled Boomers, the idea of revisiting the 1960s is appealing, precisely because they feel they might have missed out the first time around.)

Boomers often comment that their own parents 'seemed old' by the time they were in their forties whereas the Boomers insist that, at the same age, they still feel young, vital, attractive and 'sexual'. (It might come as a shock to members of the Lucky Generation to find that their Boomer offspring assume they were sexually dead by the time they had reached middle age. Perhaps their response would be to say that they didn't feel the same need to flaunt it as the Boomers seem to.)

All of this is potentially rather distasteful to the Boomers' children. At the time when they are coming into adolescence and young adulthood and becoming actively involved in love and courtship, it is sometimes an embarrassment to find that one or both of their parents are engaged in parallel pursuits. (The embarrassment can be particularly acute if a divorced father is pursuing a younger woman who is not much older than his own daughter.) But, for a generation hooked on nostalgia, nostalgic recollections of falling in love are one of the most potent forces keeping elastic adolescence at full stretch.

Yet all this determination to 'stay young' and to nurture strong nostalgic links with their own youth is its own kind of burden and makes its own contribution to the reported stress levels among Boomers. For all their quest for fun, the Boomers are acutely conscious of their own anxieties and disappointments as the world has turned out to be darker and more complex than they expected it to be. They acknowledge that their frequent retreat into alcohol, tranquillisers and other drugs is a means of easing the pain. 'Why does it all have to be so hard?' is a question often asked by those trying to come to terms with the difficulties of a second or third marriage, the strain of raising someone else's children, and the challenge of finding a job after a painful retrenchment.

WANTED: TAMPONS WITH BEEPERS

Needless to say, Boomers generally do not attribute their preoccupation with stress to the broad sweep of world events; they don't acknowledge that the Cold War taught them to live in a state of underlying tension. Their focus is more narrow, more personal and more immediate than that. They refer to the impact of divorce, the increasing complexity of life in a household where both parents are working, the uncertainty of employment for them or their children and, more generally, a sense of shortness of time which makes them feel like victims of contemporary life.

The idea of stress is inextricably connected in their minds to the idea of busyness and that, in turn, seems to be essentially a problem of time. Indeed, to hear Boomers talk, it sounds as if time has become the most precious commodity of the nineties:

Our lives are getting so busy, I reckon they will have to invent tampons with some sort of beeper on them, to let you know when to change them. We are so busy, we forget. I feel as if I am on this merry-go-round and I can't get off – it goes round and round and one day just flows into the next. Life has become harder for us because we try to fit so much into every day. My mother never went to work, so what she did while we were at school, I have to fit in after work. And there weren't all these things for kids to be involved in.

Being a sole parent makes it harder, too. You are trying to do a whole lot of things at once. I really would like to have a bit more time . . . it's even more important to me than having more money.

Boomers believe that their lives are much more complicated than their parents' were. Although they would rarely wish to turn back the clock and lead the kind of lives their parents led, there is a touch of envy in their nostalgic reflections on the simplicity of family life as they recall it from their own childhoods.

Complexity, in fact, turns out to be one of the most significant factors in Boomers' own diagnosis of the causes of their stress. Their personal lives often seem increasingly complex – partly because of the rapid rise in the divorce rate and the extraordinary challenges posed by trying to maintain the momentum of life in fractured or blended families.

But complexity is also associated with their children's lives. In a typical Boomer marriage, both partners are working and one of the ways they have found of managing their scarce resources of time for parenting is to structure their children's lives more tightly. So Boomer parents typically report that even though they might not spend as much time just 'being with' their children as their own parents did with them, they seem to spend much more time *organising* their children's activities, and ferrying them to and fro.

Occasionally, Boomers ponder the fact that they must have wanted to do this; they must have intended to organise their lives – and their children's lives – to be as busy and complex as they are. Some concession is even made to the possibility that they thrive on stress:

I'm not unhappy with my life. It's hectic, but that's partly by choice. I wouldn't like it any other way. I like the experiences

I'm having and the exposure to a variety of things, and I like to be busy. I don't want to slow down. I believe that what we are doing is best for my children and I am sure they are having a far more stimulating and interesting time than I had as a child. Still, I sometimes wonder if we would all be better off with a simpler way of life . . .

That wistful comment about 'a simpler way of life' pops up whenever Boomers take stock of their fast-paced, complex and stressful lives:

Life is far too busy at the moment. We live a much faster life than our parents did. It was much calmer when women didn't work, everything was delivered, and children didn't have so many organised activities. Life is much more stressful now – I feel as though I'm constantly on the road.

For me, even mowing the lawn has become a type of meditation and a way to unwind and get rid of the stress.

When husband and wife both work, they don't have time to spend with each other or with the kids. Consequently, someone is likely to be unhappy in the relationship. My husband and I do have conversations, but less than we used to and they are almost always about the kids, the house or money. I hear a lot of women saying they don't have time to talk to their husband. Frankly, I look forward to retirement – isn't that dreadful? I'm looking forward to the day when we can be together and have some quality time for each other because at the moment we don't – it's all rush, rush, rush.

Not surprisingly, given their sense of time's scarcity and life's complexity, many Boomers report that a midlife crisis is upon them. Coming to the middle of lives which they had expected to be comfortable, happy and even prosperous, they often find themselves plagued by feelings of uncertainty and insecurity, and by the sense of inadequate resources to cope with these feelings. Perhaps most people harbour such feelings as they pass the probable midpoint of their lives but, for Boomers, the crisis is exacerbated by a strong sense of disappointment, rooted in their experience of the sixties. The over-promise of that decade could never have been fulfilled, but the sense of hopes having been dashed is especially poignant for a generation whose expectations were so high:

> *You ask yourself, what is the point of all this? Why are we all rushing about? There must be more to life than this. I hear my wife saying to the kids that Daddy is having his midlife crisis, but I don't think she realises that it is true. Sometimes I just feel like walking away from the whole thing.*
>
> *I'm sure my father didn't have a midlife crisis. His life was much more calm and much more organised. I seem to lurch from crisis to crisis, but this one [retrenchment] is the worst. I can't even rely on job security any more.*

If Boomers were a symbol of their parents' return to peace and contentment after the horrors of World War II, peace and contentment are far from being the hallmarks of the Boomers themselves. Although they acknowledge that they are, in many ways, significantly better off than their parents were – better educated, more affluent, less rigid in their attitudes – and although they believe that life might be even tougher for their children than it has been for them, they are still in the mood to complain.

If Boomers could wave a magic wand over their lives, they would want to reduce stress and the way they would like to do it would be by stretching time – allowing them to continue to do all the things they do, but to do them at a slower pace. Since no such wand is available, Boomers face the classic dilemma: am I serious about wanting to introduce more simplicity into my life, or have I learned to thrive on stress? While they strive to resolve that dilemma, they are on the alert for news of the next stress-reliever: tranquillisers, yoga, meditation, New Age spirituality, jogging, or a new frontier of sexual ecstasy.

SHIFTING SANDS: MARRIAGE AND WORK

The Boomers are a generation in search of peace of mind. In spite of their perception that, in material terms, they have done better than their parents did, they are still coming to terms with the fact that their parents' confidence – expressed in a certain calmness of outlook – continues to elude them.

Some of them believe that their feelings of insecurity and anxiety are simply characteristic of *anyone*'s middle years (even though they are inclined to think that the midlife crisis is more commonplace today than it was when their parents were at the same stage in the life cycle). More generally, though, they believe that they are the victims of such radical changes in Australian society that they have been forced to rethink their values, their priorities, and their aspirations at a time in their lives when they had expected to be enjoying a greater sense of freedom and a greater sense of control over their future.

They look back at their parents' generation and marvel at the routines and rituals which shaped and defined their parents' lives. The idea of Monday being washing day and Friday being shopping day seems both impossibly quaint and curiously desirable. Boomers envy their parents for having lived at a time when 'things seemed more cut-and-dried' and when even personal morality seemed more straightforward than it does in the kaleidoscopic world of relativity and post-modernism. There is some uncertainty about whether a shifting set of values (or even a retreat into materialism as a self-contained ethic) might have created the pressures and uncertainties of contemporary life, or whether it is the other way around: has the increasing complexity of contemporary life rendered 'yesterday's values' obsolete?

Without devoting too much of their time to that debate, Boomers do believe that the fundamental characteristic of contemporary Australian life is its instability: everything from multiculturalism and republicanism to feminism and environmentalism challenges previous ways of thinking about life in Australia: these postwar babies never expected to have to live with such constant uncertainty – Australia's and their own.

In amongst all the uncertainties arising from gender-role confusion, the discovery that children are becoming more demanding and assertive than ever, and an uneasiness about Australia's emerging cultural identity, there are two over-riding factors which combine to make Boomers feel unsure of themselves. Although most of them are married and in paid employment, they are troubled by the sense that those twin pillars of the social order – stable families and stable jobs – are crumbling.

Marriage and the family

Marriage for the Lucky Generation might not have been blissful, but at least it was stable. Marriage was one of the institutions which served as a reference point for defining the Australian way of life. It was taken for granted that the vast majority of adults would marry and that those marriages would remain intact – for better or worse – in the same way as marriages had for their own parents.

But all that changed in the transition from the Lucky Generation to the baby-boom generation. One of the clearest signs of the emerging 'generation gap' was that the Boomers began to adopt a quite different view of marriage from that of their parents. They started talking about the quality of the relationship. They sought personal happiness in the context of marriage. They turned the spotlight on the dynamics of marriage in a way which their parents and grandparents would rarely have dreamed of doing. ('How do you mean, your *relationship*,' their parents might ask. 'You're married, aren't you?') Because the Boomers were jettisoning many of their parents' values – including values associated with sexual morality – they were quite comfortable with the symbolism of a new view of marriage.

In the event, the Boomers have turned out to be the most divorced generation in Australia's history (and, for the first time in our history, the majority of divorces are being initiated by women). Their children's divorce rate may well turn out to exceed theirs, but the Boomers have shocked their own parents by their rate of marriage breakdown, pioneering new patterns of marriage and divorce in Australian society. They know that they have revolutionised the institution, and they acknowledge that the instability of marriage creates its own broader sense of uncertainty.

Of course, new approaches to marriage mean new approaches to parenting and family life. When Australia observed the United Nations' International Year of the Family in 1994, the occasion was marked by 12 months of wrangling about an acceptable definition of 'the family', and no wonder: step-families, blended families, one-parent families, families based on *de facto* marriages as well as legal marriages – all of these groupings add their own dimensions to the meaning of the term 'family' and all of them are acknowledged as legitimate and, indeed, part of the mainstream of contemporary Australian family life. With almost one million dependent children living with just one parent, the time has long since passed when the one-parent family might be thought of as 'fringe' or 'experimental': the one-parent family is as 'normal' as the two-parent family.

Radical changes in the patterns of marriage, divorce, family formation and dislocation are inextricably linked to radical changes in the Boomers' understanding of the roles and responsibilities of men and women. The Boomers have been in the thick of the gender revolution and the oldest of the Boomer women were among the pioneers in redefining what it means to be a woman in Australian society. In particular, it is the Boomer generation who have insisted on a woman's right to *equality*; on the right of every woman to have a fully developed sense of personal identity and the status of an independent person.

But the shift from women as second-class citizens to the concept of equality between men and women has not been painless; nor is the process over. Along the way, new strains have been imposed on many Boomer marriages as unwilling males have been slow to understand what 'equality' really means, and slow to accept that their wives' demands for equality in every aspect of their lives were serious. Indeed, it is fair to say that, from the point of view of Boomer men, one of the great sources of stress and insecurity in relation to marriage has been their inability (or reluctance) to appreciate the full implications and ramifications of the women's liberation movement.

Once the divorce rate is known to have risen above 30 per cent, it is inevitable that people who might previously not have thought about divorce – including those who describe themselves as being happily married – will think about it. Divorce has become part of the Boomers' social reality, encouraging people to be more critical of the quality of their own marriages. A divorce within an extended family or within a group of friends will have a kind of 'ripple effect', causing other members of the social network to examine their own marriages in a different way.

In fact, it is likely that about 65 per cent of Boomer marriages will remain intact. But the *attitude* to marriage and divorce has changed so radically during their adult lives that there is an atmosphere which encourages the thought of divorce as a possibility. Marriage is a different state of mind from the way it was for their parents. Even if a marriage turns out to be permanent, there is tacit acceptance of the possibility of its failure: Boomers no longer assume that, come what may, marriages will be preserved and protected.

So there is a kind of 'what if . . .' mentality operating just below the level of consciousness in the minds of many Boomer spouses, even when their marriages are successful and seem likely to survive. A generation whose women have embraced the idea of freedom of choice with such enthusiasm is bound to be a generation whose marriages are put under a microscope: 'I can choose,' says a typical Boomer woman, 'whether to go on with this or not; I am not locked in; I am not trapped.'

I think quite often about whether my marriage will survive. It probably won't, but I hope it will. There is a sort of insecurity about marriage today that I know my parents' generation didn't have to face. In many ways, it's a good thing, but it does make you more anxious.

Most of my friends got married about 20 or 21 and I was best man eight times in a short period of time. Not one of them is still with that first wife . . . most have remarried. There doesn't seem to be the commitment there that I saw in my parents' marriage.

I'm not thinking about retirement yet. Things change . . . people change as you get older. It depends on whether my wife and I will still be together. We were friendly with five couples and we had a nice group going. But all the others are divorced now. We are the only ones still together.

It is not simply the new view of marriage as a less stable institution which breeds a feeling of insecurity among Boomers; it is also the fact that they often feel uncertain about whether the moves they have made – especially involving divorce and remarriage – have actually been worth the trauma and struggle, particularly for their children. Boomers, like most people, yearn for happy and stable marriages and they share an almost universal belief that divorce must adversely affect the well-being of children, at least to some extent, even though they desperately hope it hasn't done so in the case of their own. They acknowledge that most of their contemporaries would not be prepared to stay together 'for the sake of the children' if their marriages were unsatisfactory, yet those who have been through divorce often wonder whether they have made guinea pigs of their own children in some vast social experiment.

In her book *Promiscuities*, Naomi Woolf explores that same question from the child's point of view:

Adults, in an affluent country that had been premised on the notion of delaying gratification for the sake of one's children, began to put their own gratification first; and the children were left to accommodate the second infancy of the grown-ups. Often, we became our parents' parents.[9]

The institution of marriage has had a rocky history in Australia, even before the Boomers got hold of it. Before World War II, approximately 20 per cent of Australian adults never married or had children. In 1901, there were more one-parent families than there are now (though, as Dr Don Edgar, founding director of the Australian Institute of Family Studies, has remarked, the difference is that in those one-parent families, the other parent had probably died rather than having left the family home through separation or divorce). But it is the Boomers who so radically and determinedly shook the foundations of the institution that had been handed down to them by their own parents.

Needless to say, Boomers are strong and confident defenders of what has happened to the institution of marriage while it has been in their keeping. They will argue passionately that divorce is preferable to the perpetuation of an unhappy marriage. They will try to convince themselves that children are less damaged by divorce than by living with parents who don't love each other (or don't love each other *enough*). In particular, they will defend the model of a family with both parents working on the grounds that this buys significant opportunities (especially educational opportunities) for their children and that it provides their children with stimulating and interesting parents. The stay-at-home mothers of the Lucky Generation, though appreciated by their children at the time, are now inclined to be stereotyped by them as having been rather limited.

While the debate rages about good marriages versus bad marriages, about staying together versus splitting up, about whether to bother with marriage at all, the undeniable truth appears to be that Boomers' anxieties have been fed by a profound insecurity about marriage. Even those who are proud of their divorces (because they see them as a sign of independence and a tangible expression of their determination to 'be happy') acknowledge that a high emotional price is paid whenever a relationship designed to be permanent turns out to be temporary:

> *I can't say I don't think about it. I do. We will probably stay together, but you can't be sure. What's a happy marriage? We tolerate each other and live on happy memories. We are exceptions to the modern rule.*

Work

For a generation that grew up in the heady days of postwar full employment, the 1970s, 1980s and 1990s have been a terrible shock. A Boomer born in 1950 was getting his or her career established in the early 1970s, just when unemployment hit five per cent in a decade where it was to average 2.5 per cent. Ten years later, when that Boomer was into his or her thirties and getting established in the family home, unemployment hit ten per cent (in a decade where it was to average five per cent). During the early 1990s, unemployment rose to sickening heights and seems likely to average around ten per cent for the decade.

(Those figures are, of course, the official unemployment figures, based on people who are actively looking for work, and excluding those who have given up. It is generally assumed that *true* unemployment levels are much higher than the official figures would suggest – perhaps even as much as twice as high.)

If adjustment to the new insecurity of marriage has been painful, then adjusting to an uncertain supply of work has more or less guaranteed an intensified state of anxiety.

For many people, the combination of marriage and a job has traditionally defined the sense of a personal identity. As Boomers approach the end of the century, they are having to learn a lesson which their parents did not have to learn: that personal identity needs to be rooted in something less transient than marriage (when the divorce rate is high) or work (when, even for those with apparently secure jobs, the possibility of unemployment has the menacing quality of a distant war-drum).

Not all Boomers wished to emulate the extraordinary stability of their fathers' careers – especially those who remained with one organisation throughout their working lives – yet they grew up with the expectation that such stability was possible. Having discovered in their middle years that, boring or not, such a prospect has receded, Boomer men in particular have had to face a significant reappraisal of the role of work. They have been challenged not only by the uncertainty of employment, but also by the feminisation of the workplace and the realisation that their wives – and other women – have enthusiastically entered the workforce in the quest for the sense of identity and personal liberation previously available mainly to men. (It's not just that a largely male domain has been invaded; it's also that 'secret men's business' – the knowledge that work can be deeply satisfying and even fun – has been exposed.)

Many Boomer men have been forced to rethink not only the role of work in their lives but also their own roles as 'chief bread-winner'. In most two-adult Boomer households, the male is still earning more money than the female (and is more likely to have full-time work), but the shift from a one-income culture to a two-income culture has been radical:

> *I never thought I would have to live with this awful feeling of insecurity about work. I always thought I was set. But so many of my friends have been retrenched or have taken voluntary redundancy . . . it makes you think. I could be in an entirely different position tomorrow.*

> *I'm actually working towards becoming a house-husband, because I don't see any future where I am. My wife can earn more than me so that may be the preferred option.*

> *Life is about the unforeseen. Being in the workforce is not easy . . . they are culling people out everywhere. There's the tension of being on the hitlist – not just for the over-fifties, but a cross-section of ages. To us, the recession has been an adversity which has been a learning experience – especially for the children . . . learning that you have to be careful with money. After 21 years, I never thought retrenchment could happen to me.*

Even if the prospect of actual unemployment does not loom large, the possibility of having to make significant career changes can be almost as unsettling:

> *I never thought I would have to change my career. I liked what I did and I am good at my work. But even though I am prepared*

to work for a lot less money, I would be lucky to get another job in the same industry. You have got to be realistic . . . you have got to go where the work is, whether you like it or not.

My career path has hit a brick wall. I now find myself wondering what I should be doing. Should I be totally changing direction . . . and to what? And is the same thing going to happen in another ten years? I think the jobs all of us are going to be doing in the future are just starting to emerge now, because the whole of society seems to be changing.

It is not only marriage and work that generate such feelings of uncertainty among Boomers. Both men and women continue to be confused about gender roles as they continue to negotiate and redefine their responsibilities.

Even though few Boomers – women *or* men – would expect to return to the gender roles and responsibilities which created such simplicity and predictability for their parents, there is nevertheless a hankering for a greater sense of clarity and a greater sense of certainty. Twenty-five years after Women's Lib unleashed such revolutionary forces in Australian society, a lot of detailed work remains to be done before Boomers know precisely what it means to be a man or a woman in the circumstances – at home and, especially, at work – in which they now find themselves.

For women in particular, the discovery that gender role issues are still alive creates feelings of tension and disappointment. Since the central message of the women's movement ('A woman is a fully-fledged person, too') seems so self-evident and straightforward, the effort that has been needed to express that principle in daily life has been surprising, perplexing, exhausting – and sometimes infuriating:

I'm concerned about what my children are going to do when they get to being husbands and wives. There is no set role for a man or a woman . . . that is just going to have to be the accepted thing. Men's roles have changed more than women's, and men are still finding it very hard. They don't really know where they stand. Some of my friends think I'm a bit mean expecting so much from my husband – like him making dinner for us one night a week. I went away with a girlfriend and our kids for a week recently, and she made meals for her husband for each day and put them in the freezer. She couldn't stop mothering. She thought I was mean for not doing it for my husband. She tried to make me out to be the one that's odd.

There's yet another aspect of family life which causes anxiety for Boomers and which distinguishes them from their parents' generation: fear for the safety of their children.

Boomers believe that they are the first generation of Australians who have had to face the ever-present worry about the welfare, whereabouts and well-being of their children. To some extent, they attribute this to the increase in the number of working mothers, implying that there is less after-school supervision of children at home. But they also attribute it to a decline in the sense of community in local neighbourhoods and a feeling that there are more 'strange people' about, who may not be entirely benevolent in their attitudes towards children.

Like virtually every chip in the mosaic of Boomer attitudes and concerns, fear for the safety of one's children is connected to a number of other attitudes. The link between worry about children and the rise of the working mother is the most obvious of these connections, but Boomer parents also believe that the rather frantic pace of their own lives leaves them insufficient time and energy for parental activity and this heightens their anxieties about what their children are doing in unsupervised hours. That concern, in turn, fuels the urge to create more supervised activities for their children, adding further momentum to the pace of their own lives.

There is a connection, too, between the lurking fear of unemployment and fear for the safety of children: Boomers wonder whether the rise of unemployment among young adults has made such a significant contribution to vandalism and vagrancy that it creates a menace in any local neighbourhood, as aimless adolescents and young adults look for ways to fill in the time – perhaps seeking something to do for 'kicks'. (On reflection, Boomers sometimes concede that their fears are exaggerated, and they admit that the incidence of attacks on children – kidnapping, assault, abuse – is far lower than their fear would suggest. Nevertheless, the fear is real enough, if only as a projection of deeper anxieties onto a seemingly 'rational' concern):

> *We used to go down to the park and play . . . we used to roam far and wide after school. Everyone's mothers were at home and the whole place was probably safe. These days, I would never let my kids go down to the park unsupervised. I even insist that they must stay in the back yard – not the front – when they get home from school, until I get home. That's a big change from my parents' generation. We worry a lot more about our children's safety than our parents did. I'm sure it wasn't an issue for them, but it is certainly an issue for me.*

Wherever they look, Baby Boomers see trouble. The sense of stress which permeates their lives has raised their anxiety levels and caused them to seek out 'worry targets' which can justify their sense of uneasiness.

This is not as irrational as it might seem, however, since we are talking about a generation who have been living through one of the most profound periods of redefinition and reorientation in Australia's social, cultural and economic history. This generation initially revelled in the 'generation gap': as they hit their middle years, they have no desire to close that cultural gap between their own generation and their parents', yet there is a palpable sense of strain at having to play the pioneering role of people who are reinventing their own society.

Dr Don Edgar has graphically described the shaking of the foundations of the Boomers' security:

> Australia is facing the same family dilemma as many other Western industrial nations . . . The demands of the economy and working life are tearing apart family life as we have known it. Solutions to Australians' economic woes may demand tight

monetary policies and control of inflation but the real impact is in house prices, bank and business collapses, rising unemployment for family members, scarce and expensive child-care and an increasingly 'targeted' definition of social justice which splits society even further into the haves and have-nots . . . [10]

Family life and working life are never easy to separate. When both of them simultaneously experience the seismic shock of social change, this is a double whammy. Boomers know that all too well.

'IT ALL SEEMS SO SERIOUS'

For a generation that saw themselves as iconoclastic, rebellious and determined to celebrate their escape from the straitjacket of old-fashioned mores, the Boomers have been surprised to find that, as they reach their middle years, life is more earnest than they had expected it to be and, in many ways, they find themselves under pressure to *be good* (responsible parents, skilful lovers, sensitive employers, informed voters, careful of the environment, 'politically correct' in language and attitude, 'aware' consumers).

In contrast with their parents' generation – who were pleasantly surprised by the way their lives turned out – Boomers are discovering that life is harder than they expected it to be; that the 'peace and love' of the 1960s has turned into tension and stress in the 1990s; that their beloved freedom has given way to a feeling of being enclosed by responsibilities, pressures and anxieties.

If life does seem unexpectedly serious and difficult for the Boomers, then at least part of the explanation might lie in the fact that they were the children and young adolescents of the Swinging Sixties. Rock-and-roll music, the explosion of satirical humour, sexual permissiveness *(Hooray for the pill!)*, the mining and stock-market boom, the emergence of a drug subculture with its hippies and flower children, the 'God-is-dead' debate, the man-on-the-moon space race, the shadowy tensions of the Cold War, and even the shock of John F. Kennedy's assassination created an exciting and eventful context for the Boomers' early development. Life seemed dramatic, stimulating, liberating and full of potential. Even dark events like the Vietnam War became the focus of exuberant demonstrations: this was a generation whose early trademark was exuberance. The effectiveness of their anti-war demonstrations was also a powerful sign to them that, in matters large and small, they could make their mark; have their own way; change the world.

The Vietnam War sent mixed signals to the generation who so trenchantly opposed it: when it was over, the Americans and their allies clearly hadn't won, but neither were they quite prepared to concede that they'd lost. In effect, they'd quit. The ambiguity of the situation (and the murkiness of the politics involved) was a harbinger of Boomers' later feelings of uncertainty and cynicism; at the time, it was primarily an encouragement to them to step up the pace of their lives while the going was good. Vietnam reinforced the Boomers' unwelcome conviction that a nuclear war between the superpowers remained possible. It also fuelled a growing conviction that America was not necessarily either heroic or invincible.

The whole experience of Vietnam heightened Boomers' sense of mistrust of the older generation and stimulated their iconoclastic view of themselves: 'if the world is going to be made a better, safer place, it will be up to us'. The slogan *Make love, not war* seemed like a good place to start. Steadily increasing material prosperity made its own contribution to this rather buoyant sense that 'the world is our oyster'.

Against that background, the Boomers' middle years might seem, quite understandably, to be heavy going. Life is still turbulent, but the excitement and exuberance seem to have given way to the dawning of a sober understanding of what is entailed in adult responsibility. There is a certain grimness about this generation's attitude even towards marriage and parenting which reveals the trouble they have had in coming to terms with the pressures of their middle years. Although they constantly describe themselves as being better parents than their own parents were, they still sometimes acknowledge the need to 'force themselves' to spend time with their children, and they are conscious of the pressure to be 'a good parent':

I have had to face the fact that decisions I make for myself affect the rest of the family. I'm locked into a position of not being able to pursue all the wants I have. As I left the house tonight, with one child in tears over maths homework and the other two fighting, I said, 'Do you know where I'd rather be going tonight? The pictures and then out to dinner . . . but where am I going? To a fundraising meeting at the school, because of you three.'

I didn't anticipate not getting my own way in a marriage. I really didn't realise that there were so many other things to consider, other than myself. When I think of women I know who have recently been divorced, I think of women who have been trying to find themselves. Our parents' generation were all for their families, because they had nowhere else to go. Now, it's easier: if you are in a troubled relationship, you can walk out.

I do love the kids, but they put a big strain on your marriage – financially, emotionally, sexually. By the time you've finished with them, you're too tired for anything with your husband. Our mothers might have seemed less selfish, but I think we do a lot more with our kids. The pressure is on parents, especially mothers, to spend time with our children. Always in the back of my mind, I feel guilty if I sit down and do something I want to do. I think, 'I should be devoting this spare hour to Jason . . .'

Perhaps the Boomers expect to be stressed as a direct consequence of having stretched their adolescence beyond its accepted limit. When they talk about their 'responsible parenting', it sometimes sounds as if they are trying to compensate for having remained carefree and irresponsible for as long as they possibly could.

Whatever the explanation, there is no doubt that Boomers believe they are taking the parenting task more seriously than their own parents did. Given the busyness and complexity of lives in a household where both parents are working, or a one-parent family with a working parent, it is perhaps inevitable that the rituals and routines of parenting would need to be carefully programmed. But parenting is never an entirely predictable process: crises are bound to occur frequently, but never according to any plan or pattern. For Boomer parents (especially working mothers) whose lives are already complex and hurried, such crises can seem disproportionately disruptive and traumatic because they upset a fairly delicate balance. (*But you simply have to go to your father's this weekend: I'm going away . . . No, you can't have your friends over tonight: I have to prepare for an important meeting in the morning . . . Don't tell me your problems just now: I'm whacked.*)

Hence, the need for *quality time*. It is a common theme among Boomer parents that, since they don't seem to have *enough* time to spend with their children, they want to make the available time count. So they speak of the 'quality time' which is available to them when they are driving one of their children to or from a sporting event or a music lesson. They speak of a Sunday morning breakfast as time 'set aside' for the family. Or they speak of their determination to spend half an hour with the children at bedtime.

'Quality time' is a term with a rather plaintive connotation. It sounds like parents desperate to make up for lost time and, in the process, rolling another burden of stress onto their shoulders. Children, of course, soon learn to detect the quality time glint in their parents' eyes and to duck for cover when they can see a burst of quality time coming.

The quality time spotlight is too emotionally intense. When the concept of quality time is made explicit, it forces parents and children to focus on the dynamics of family life and, rather like thinking too hard about what is involved in walking or riding a bicycle, that can easily cause the process to come unstuck.

But it is typical of Boomers to be earnest about parenting because, as they reach their middle years, they are inclined to become more earnest about everything: caring for the environment, avoiding sexist language, voting responsibly, being politically correct. Though it sounds like the ultimate contradiction of the early attitudes of the Boomers, it is actually quite consistent: when they decide that it is time to act like grown-ups, they tackle that with the same impatience and intensity as they have tackled everything else:

My wife and I have a very good sex life because we both put some effort into it.

When we grew up, we were terrified of nuclear war. But now that threat has passed and the main worries are environmental pollution and over-population. There have been times in my life when I've regretted having the three kids, but I have decided to try and be more positive, for their sake.

There's no romance in my life any more. Circumstances change you. I'm not the happy-go-lucky person I used to be.

The trouble is, we know so much more about parenting these days. When we were growing up, they didn't have to give every type of behaviour a name.

This is more a 'responsibility and worry' stage of life. There is more than just yourself to answer to.

Previous generations might also have expressed sentiments like these, but, looking back, the Lucky Generation certainly believe they simply 'got on with it'. They are bemused by their Boomer offspring's solemn commitment to navel-gazing, to self-analysis and to the relentless pursuit of personal gratification. Life might be turning out to be tougher than Boomers had been led to expect, but they are still tempted by the view that, if they can just organise things a little better or put in a little more effort, happiness will come to them.

One reason why Boomers are finding life tougher than they believe it was for their parents at the same stage in the life cycle is that many of them are having their children later than their parents did (especially if it is a 'second crop' from a second marriage); their children are staying at home for longer (or leaving and then coming back); and their parents are living longer and therefore requiring care and support. Indeed, one of the emerging cries of Boomers is that they are caught in the middle of caring for two generations at once.

In a 1995 report to the Department of Employment, Education, Training and Youth Affairs entitled *I go to work for a holiday*, Dr Elizabeth Watson of the University of Western Sydney described many working women as being torn between their need to care for ageing parents and their need to maintain their own careers: 'They are trying to do two major tasks – remain responsible workers and do the right thing by their employers, but also to provide the best care it was possible to provide for their parents. This can create enormous stress and an enormous toll on their health.'

This feeling of being responsible for two generations at once, while trying to lead 'fulfilling' lives of their own, breeds understandable resentment. Some Boomers quip that they are likely to die from exhaustion before their parents do, because they are carrying the double burden of caring for their children *and* their parents, or, in the case of Boomer women, it is often a triple burden because they are carrying the working-mother load as well:

> Now I think about it, I realise my mother actually had quite an easy time. She was supported by my father and she was a devoted mother, but we were all off her hands by the time we were in our early twenties. She had plenty of time for voluntary work, or gardening, or whatever she wanted to do. She criticises me for rushing around like a scalded cat, but she is part of the reason. She needs more care now she is getting old and I am still juggling the children as well. Plus the job on top of that . . . sometimes I feel like the most unliberated woman on earth. I just don't have the energy for all this. I wonder if the time will ever come when I can play the gracious lady. I doubt it . . . and I don't suppose I really want to be like that, in my heart.

Boomers were determined to make it up as they went along. They wanted to break the mould into which their parents and grandparents had fitted with such apparent comfort. They wanted to reject their parents' values and to challenge the institutions and conventions which enshrined those values. They were determined to lead more liberated and more fulfilling lives. They believed in 'the power of love' in a way which their parents would have regarded as somewhat self-indulgent, and their children as sentimental.

And now they are paying a heavy price. They feel their responsibilities with the keenness of a person who thought that life was going to be a breeze and for whom the prospect of turning 50 was almost inconceivable – until it finally happened to the oldest of the Boomers in 1996. (As Erica Jong put it: 'How did we get to be the grown-ups?')

Have the rebels of the sixties become the wowsers of the nineties? That might be going too far, but when you consider that it is Boomers who are leading the charge for tougher censorship, Boomers who were in the vanguard of the political correctness movement and Boomers who are busily finding new ways of 'regulating' society – through anti-vilification laws, compulsory super-annuation, anti-smoking regulations and corporate codes of practice – it is certainly safe to say that the Boomers are caught up in a major rethink. Listening to them worrying about their own children and sounding as if they distrust anyone under the age of 30, it is hard to remember that this is the generation of tearaways for whom the term 'generation gap' had to be invented to describe their reluctance to conform to their parents' style and standards. This is the generation that once distrusted anyone *over* 30.

THE MALE FOCUS: LOSING 'CONTROL'

If you are looking for confirmation of the theory that men and women never see the world in quite the same way, look no further than the Boomers. Male and female Boomers share their concern with stress, and they share a desire to simplify their lives, to slow down and to find 'quality time' (for themselves, as well as for their children). But there are some big gender differences. Whereas women of this generation are fundamentally concerned with establishing their freedom to choose how to express the notion of sexual equality, male Boomers typically feel that, compared with their fathers' generation, their sense of power and control has been eroded, at home and at work. They are no longer automatically expected to be in charge in either place, simply because they are men, and their adjustment to that realisation has been slow and sometimes painful.

However unrealistically, Boomer men now in their middle years recall their fathers' lives at the same stage of the life cycle as having been full of clarity, purpose, hard work, confidence and security. They believe their fathers had more leisure than they do, more personal privacy, more 'time out', and more freedom to indulge their own pursuits (whether it was drinking, golf or working late). They believe their fathers enjoyed more respect from their children (and from their wives) than Boomer fathers do today.

No doubt such recollections are rose-tinted by nostalgia, yet Boomer fathers typically insist that they lack many of those things enjoyed by their own fathers – even though they have a generally higher standard of living and a far better level of education.

The Boomer male in his middle years is likely to feel that he lacks his father's confidence about the future and that, in contrast to his father's drive to distance himself from a deprived and difficult past, he is keen to hold onto the symbols and promises of his adolescence and young adulthood. He believes that his life is less stable, that his role as husband and father is less clear-cut and that his position in the workforce is not likely to be as secure as his father's was (partly because of the growing presence of 'competitive women' at work).

It is easy to understand why men who grew up at a time when their fathers were automatically regarded as the head of the household and the breadwinner should feel rather threatened by the contemporary challenge to those central features of traditional, masculine status. But the male sense of losing control seems even more deeply rooted than that. It is the outcome of having lived through the turbulent years of the gender revolution when the women's liberation movement was not simply redefining the place of women but, by implication, challenging traditional notions of gender in contemporary society.

Boomer women had plenty to rebel against, as they responded to the evocative messages of feminism. Boomer men, by contrast, were not conscious of any need to rebel on gender issues at all. For them, the model of the dominant male was perfectly satisfactory and they had every reason to look forward to inheriting their fathers' mantle.

But that was not to be.

In the event, the males of the baby-boom generation were destined to feel like guinea pigs in an experiment in which they would be asked to abandon the expectations created for them by their fathers and grandfathers about what it should mean to be a man in Australia. Not all of them would agree to take part, but virtually all of them would be affected by the fallout from that experiment (which was not, of course, an experiment at all; it was a revolution).

As Boomer males moved towards their middle years, they came to realise that they were the largely involuntary participants in that revolution. Unlike an experiment, there would never be a moment when someone could decide to call it off and put things back the way they used to be.

As teenage rebels and young-adult iconoclasts, Boomer men were happy to flout convention and to challenge the values and beliefs of their parents' generation. They wanted to break the mould; to assert the new order; to widen the generation gap. Their music said it, their clothes said it, their language said it, their sexual behaviour said it and their materialism said it. But there was no way for them to know that their sisters, girlfriends and wives had iconoclasm of a totally different order in mind. They couldn't have known, on their journey through the Swinging Sixties, that 'sexual equality' was going to mean something far more than sharing drugs with your girlfriend or expecting women to take as many sexual initiatives as men, or even acknowledging that girls had as much right to secondary and tertiary education as boys had. In fact, sexual equality would mean something far more profound: it would ask Boomer men to rethink the meaning of masculinity.

Boomer boys were direct descendants of a hunter-gatherer culture. Although the Industrial Revolution had effectively brought village life to an end and spawned the suburbs of great industrial towns and cities (where the residents were separated both from their work and from the land which ultimately sustained them), the relative positions of men and women did not change immediately. The 'hunting and gathering' became progressively more symbolic as men sought employment in factories and offices, rather than in grazing and agriculture, but the man was still the breadwinner whose domain lay primarily in the world of work; the woman was typically the housewife whose domain lay primarily in the world of child-care and domesticity. The man was unequivocally the head of the household and the distinction between men's work and women's work was easily made by a culture which was still evolving from its hunter-gatherer origins.

Of course, there were many exceptions to that stereotype (and many women, incidentally, who believed that *they* were the true heads of the households). But the stereotypical culture survived the journey from Europe to Australia, and the passage of time.

When the babies born in the postwar boom came to their adolescence, they were living in households which were still recognisable as contemporary suburban manifestations of a hunter-gatherer mentality. Typically, their fathers worked for wages which were sufficient to support a family which was mainly reared by the mother. The mother, typically, was an active participant in the village life of her street and suburb. She belonged to the genus 'housewife' and that involved her in a kind of communal mothering role which, in suburban Australia, often extended to automatic care and concern for neighbours' children – as they rushed into and out of her house – as well as her own. Boys learned what it meant to be a man and what it meant to be a woman from their parents' models. (Again, the necessary disclaimer: there were many exceptions, particularly in the minority of households where both parents had paid employment outside the home, but the stereotype was dominant.)

Some men raised in this culture did not enjoy it. They preferred the idea of interchangeable roles and responsibilities between men and women, and they resented the fact that their wives were entirely supported by them. Yet those men had a clear sense of what was expected of them and even drew some comfort from the belief that masculinity entailed an identifiable set of responsibilities.

The women's movement of the 1970s and 1980s challenged all that. Now, men were being asked to acknowledge the chauvinism in some of their traditional attitudes towards women. They were being asked to confess to having assigned women the status of second-class citizens (though many of them have resisted inherited guilt on this point, believing that it was their fathers and grandfathers who had operated on that assumption).

Those men who believed they had always thought of men and women as being equal were rather shocked to find that this claim was being discounted or even ridiculed by some feminists, and that many attitudes towards gender roles and responsibilities which men regarded as normal were being attacked as evidence of sexism.

Given their cultural inheritance, it is hardly surprising that Boomer men were initially destabilised and confused by the impact of the women's movement. Some of them simply blamed women for their feelings of uncertainty or inadequacy. Others expressed support for feminism but acknowledged that the process of adaptation was turning out to be slow and painful. At home and at work, Boomer men would compare their lot with that of their own fathers and conclude that, in many ways, their fathers had an easier time simply because of the relative clarity and stability of gender roles within their generation. Although many Boomers admit that their fathers didn't always deserve the position of authority which their families gave them, and although they observe that their fathers were generally insufficiently grateful for their wives' support, the Boomer son ruefully notes that he wouldn't mind a bit of the same kind of respect. A sense of male authority having been eroded is widespread, even as women continue to complain that in business and the professions, men still have the levers of power firmly in their grasp. When men say that male power is being eroded, however, they are referring to something less specific than that, and rather more profound: they sense a shift in the dynamics of male–female relationships in which the power that men are losing is not the power *over women*; they are referring to the loss of the powerful sense of understanding the male role and being in control of it. In other words, men feel that male 'identity' is shifting and until they can relocate it, they are bound to feel some confusion, uncertainty and insecurity.

This is a tacit acknowledgement of the fact that the women's movement is, after all, a *women*'s movement: part of the male confusion derives from the fact that while they are implicated in it, they are neither its initiators nor its organisers. Some of them feel as if they are its victims, but, more commonly, they feel as though they are being showered by fallout from the gender revolution without quite knowing what to do about it, or whether they have any say in what will happen next.

And yet, 25 years after the revolution began in earnest, there is an almost universal acknowledgement among Boomer males that this was a revolution which had to happen. No matter how much resentment there might be, it is almost always tinged with understanding. Conversely, no matter how much understanding there might be, it is almost always tinged with some resentment. Men have begun to accept, deep within themselves, that their fathers and grandfathers (and they themselves – especially in the sixties) did not interpret sexual equality in ways which could ever have been acceptable to women. They now acknowledge that women, responding to their rising standard of education and the rapidly awakening sense of their own potential, were bound to demand equal *status* with men, an equally authentic *sense of identity* as men's, and as firm a control over their own destiny as any man might expect to have.

This did not mean that women wanted to *be* men, nor even that most women wanted to be *like* men. What it meant was that women wanted access to the same sense of freedom and independence, the same sense of control, that had traditionally been enjoyed by men.

The fact that many of those men did not think of their lives as being characterised by freedom or control was irrelevant: the

revolution, inevitably, had to deal in stereotypes and the stereotype of the patronising, chauvinistic male was soon discovered
by feminists to be lurking just under the surface of almost every
facet of male behaviour.

Boomer feminists will probably have to wait until they can
observe the attitudes and behaviour of their grandsons before they
can feel confident about how the revolution has turned out. In the
meantime, Boomer males are making concessions which they
regard as significant – in gender etiquette, in the creation of equal
opportunities at work, and in the provision of domestic support
(especially in parenting). But they are understandably wary. They
are on red alert for any sign of hypocrisy or duplicity in the way
women are acting out the messages of feminism. 'Equal pay for
equal work', for example, is a slogan which men strongly support
provided the work is equal. 'Shared responsibilities at home' might
be an acceptable slogan to men, as long as they feel that their wives
are shouldering equal responsibilities at work. Some signs are perhaps more significant than others; some resentments run deeper
than others; some male complaints are cloaked in unconscious
irony:

> *I think I've made a lot of adjustments since my wife discovered
> women's lib, but my wife doesn't seem to have made many for
> me. For example, she knows I like schnitzel well done, but she
> never cooks it that way, even though I've reminded her time and
> again.*

To further complicate the situation, men are not at all sure that
women themselves are completely content with the way the revolution is working out. They wonder whether some of their own confusions are reflected in confusions among women. They are not
sure whether women really like 'sensitive' men, especially in bed.
While they understand that many women *say* they find the 'macho'
male to be a repugnant phenomenon, there is plenty of speculation
about whether women are actually quite attracted to macho men,
in spite of their intellectual resistance to the idea. Boomer men are

also perplexed by what they see as a shift in the focus of women's complaints: they are now likely to complain about the stress of juggling multiple roles, where they used to complain about the injustice of being relegated to the status of 'just a housewife':

> *As far as I'm concerned, women have become a bunch of whingers. They complain about how it used to be, and now they are complaining about how tough it is for them. I'm not sure they know what they want. Were they that unhappy when they were at home with the kids? My mother was at home with the kids and she was very pleased with her lot. She is proud of what she did. I can't say this to my wife, or she goes off the deep end. But I suspect she has a lot more frustration and a lot more unhappiness than my mother ever did. She has been determined to do it all her own way – her own job, her own money, her own friends – and now she bitches all day about how tough her life is. She is exhausted every weekend.*

> *You hear these feminists dolling themselves up and saying, 'I only wear make-up because I feel better'. It is as if they are scared of admitting that they might want to attract a bloke.*

Writing in the *Guardian*, Jo-Ann Goodwin confirmed what many Boomer men suspect: that Boomer women are backing away from the man who has responded too literally to the demands of the women's movement to be more sensitive, more caring, more responsible for children, and more committed to the idea of 'relationships':

You can't miss him. He doesn't even walk properly. Being so full of gender awareness, he's never sure what to do with his hips. The new man is in town. And he'll be looking for some oppressed female to offer his solidarity to. Any woman with an ounce of self-respect should walk away, briskly. A Playtex offers more satisfying support. New men came into existence in the '70s, the toxic waste of feminism. After a rough patch in the '80s, they've undergone a resurrection . . .

With badly cut boyish hair, concerned expression and a lop-sided grin that makes you want to smack his face off, the new man looks harmless. But he's a succubus. If you fall for his 'what-we-need-is-a-gynogenic-world-view' chat-up line, you will find yourself bringing up children called Dandelion and submitting to holistic massages every night.

Most new men copped on to the wheeze as an easy way to persuade naive young women on the Left to sleep with them. Unfortunately, after a while, they started to rather believe in the whole idea. Few things are better fun than talking about your-self, and being a new man opens up undreamt-of hours of enjoyable angst.

The worst of it is that these men are so unappealing, so unaes-thetic, so unsexy. Once you see through the dubious charm of someone 'who really understands women', what you are left with is a man whose clothes are appalling and who is so busy trying to be supportive he's probably forgotten what an erection is for.

Jo-Ann Goodwin's views would buck up the flagging spirits of many Boomer males who are secretly hoping that 'equality' doesn't have to involve a curious kind of androgyny in which men focus so intently on their 'feminine side' that they are no longer free to respond to their own masculinity. Jo-Ann Goodwin again:

Women are already fleeing this ghastly apparition. We need a campaign to bring back lads. Tough, arrogant and sexy, the '90s lad is not some git with a nice line in love-'em and leave-'em. He's just someone who can pass an evening without mentioning patriarchy, or expecting the Queens' Award for Industry because he cooked dinner and did the washing up.[11]

Such apparent contradictions of the conventional feminist line con-vince Boomer males that society is still in a transitional stage when it comes to gender roles and responsibilities, and this is its own kind of comfort: the proposition that 'we won't know how this is going to work itself out for another generation or so' helps to allay some of their anxieties and certainly helps to explain some of the recent hostility between men and women:

Women grew another leg and all of a sudden they got to where they should have been in the first place. But we think they've gained more than they have, because it all happened at once. Women's Lib raised a lot of eyebrows and created opposition between the sexes, but then people started to realise it was sensible. Equal opportunity is the way to go, but it has all been changing too quickly for women . . . as well as for men.

Another source of comfort for men who have found themselves caught up in the backwash of the seventies' wave of feminism is the proposition – regularly trotted out – that women are quite different from men, both biologically and psychologically, and that this makes the concept of equality very slippery indeed. As long as men take refuge in the proposition that 'women *are* different', some of them will take refuge in the idea that the women's movement is just the latest manifestation of the eternal battle of the sexes.

Indeed, one of the most fundamental of men's attitudes towards gender is that, even if it is to be conceded that everyone has *some* masculinity and *some* femininity within their make-up, such terms derive from differences between the sexes which are obvious – and which sometimes seem to create an unbridgeable gap between them. Whether men argue from biology or from a kind of cultural determinism, they come easily to the conclusion that some of the classic gender stereotypes are justified. For example, men typically continue to believe that:

• Women are 'naturals' at parenting (in a way that men aren't);

• Men have a provider/protector instinct;

• Males are more easily distracted than females (an argument now being invoked to explain girls' better performance at school);

- Women are natural worriers, whereas men are more 'relaxed';

- Women are more single-minded about what they want and more focused in pursuing it;

- Women together behave bitchily – they benefit from being 'diluted' by the presence of men;

- Men are more naturally 'active' (and more aggressive) than women;

- Women are better than men at paperwork and 'fine detail';

- Women are more enthusiastic than men about spending money;

- Women 'drag their emotions into everything';

- Women want men for company more often than men want women for company (though the reverse might be true when it comes to sex).

Such stereotypical generalisations about women are by no means the exclusive province of Boomer males, but the fact that they cite them with such relish gives some hint of the defensiveness which is still typically felt when the subject of 'equality' comes up. Equality is one thing, they say; being the same is quite another.

One of the most amusing gender differences, to Boomer men, is also a sign to them that 'women haven't changed much since my mother's generation':

The thing that always intrigues me is why women go off to the ladies' room in pairs. What do they do? Is it an excuse to get away and talk about the other people in the group? Imagine a bloke saying to another bloke, 'I'm going to the toilet – do you want to come?'

When it comes to sexual behaviour, Boomer men, who regard their generation as having been the pioneers in sexual permissiveness, have a mixed story to tell. Some of them believe that Women's Lib has resulted in women becoming sexually more aggressive and assertive, with pleasant consequences for their sexual partners. Others report that tensions over the subject of equality have translated directly into a sullen atmosphere in the bedroom in which men are disappointed to discover that their partners are expressing disapproval of them by withdrawing sexual favours:

> *Before you got married, you could get it any time you want. Once they get that ring on their finger, it slows down a bit. Well, when I say a bit . . . it's practically non-existent.*
>
> *I've tried everything with my wife – taking her out to expensive dinners, picnics in the country . . . I've even tried getting her pissed. But I've heard every excuse. If I try to give her back a rub, she tells me she's trying to sleep.*

> *I think it's done our marriage a bit of good, my wife getting dressed and going off to work every day. She gets more stimulated – who's complaining?*
>
> *When she first went back to work, she was very tired and not very interested. But now she's got into a routine, we have a terrific time. She's much more sexy than she used to be when she was just at home with the kids.*

Either way, Boomer men feel that sex is yet another area where their identities have been clouded and where some loss of control has been experienced: it might be nice to have a partner who takes the sexual initiative more often than expected, but it still requires some finetuning of the male ego.

The silver lining: fathers' relationships with their children

Whatever else they might say about the life of an Australian male at the end of the 20th century, Boomers believe that one of the most positive outcomes of the women's movement *for them* is that they have learned how to be more actively involved with their children than their own fathers were with them. The experience of being married to a woman with a job outside the home has had a big impact on the attitudes and behaviour of fathers: it has forced them to become more aware of domestic issues. This, in turn, has led some of them to be more appreciative of the significance of domestic work. (Their wives claim that awareness is one thing; action is another.)

But even those fathers who are still hesitating about making a serious commitment to cooking, cleaning and making beds are likely to be experiencing, more vividly than their fathers did, 'the joys of fatherhood'.

Men newly come to domesticity soon discover the contradictions inherent in housekeeping and even in parenting. The work is demanding and complex; the work is demeaning and trivial. The satisfactions are enormous and inexpressible, responding to the child's eternal need for nurture and formation; the satisfactions are fleeting and grotesque. Such fathers are discovering for themselves the paradox of joy and disgust involved in domestic life: the heart leaps at a child's first step, but there is even a momentary thrill to be had from a gleaming S-bend or a patch of clear floor peeping through the chaos of a child's bedroom.

The discovery of these joys has not always been spontaneous: it has often been a reaction to the scarcity of time available for parenting, and the need to share the responsibility with busy wives. Many Boomer fathers will admit to having been 'dragged into' fatherhood without any really clear idea of what their responsibilities might be and yet, under the pressure of having to step into the breach created by a working (or possibly absent) mother, men report that they start to enjoy being more active parents and take some pride in their involvement with their children.

In some cases, this leads to a renewed sense of respect for the role of mothers, although with a persistent belief that fathers can never get it 'quite right':

> *My wife went away for a long weekend with some of her girl-friends. I had the kids all to myself and I nearly went round the bend. I love them and everything, but it's hell-on-wheels trying to keep them entertained, keep the food up to them, stop the place from degenerating into a pigsty . . . I can tell you, I was incredibly relieved when my wife walked in the back door. I've never been so pleased to see her. Frankly, I don't know how single parents manage to cope.*

Yet single parents, in growing numbers, *do* manage to cope. In most cases, that parent is the mother; the father has retreated to an 'access' relationship with his children. Whether or not the absent father has remarried, he is likely to find that his parenting skills have to be sharpened up considerably if he is going to have successful access time with his children. So Boomer fathers are increasingly being pressured to become more active parents in two ways: either they are having to share the load with a working wife, or they are having to take the full load in short bursts, during periods of access to their children. It is a common theme among Boomer fathers that their own fathers would faint if they could have seen them changing nappies, feeding and bathing children, reading bed-time stories and even dutifully attending sporting events:

> *I don't think my father ever came to a single football match I played in. I have to turn up to everything. The fact is, a lot of my leisure time is spent with my children, whereas my father spent his leisure time with his mates, or on his own. I think I prefer it the way it is: there are a lot of rewards in being involved with your children, but it is very demanding as well. We're closer to our kids . . . we're more involved. Still, I wouldn't mind a bit more of the respect that we gave our fathers, or even some of the fear!*

Becoming more active parents is one thing; becoming spontaneous or willing participants in the broader range of housekeeping tasks is another:

I can't cook, I can only peel bananas.

There are two ways of pegging out the clothes – hers and mine.

The myth of the men's movement

In spite of the confusion and uncertainty which many Boomer men are experiencing during the transitional stages of their adjustment to the women's movement, there is no evidence of any significant 'men's movement' in response. Nor should one be expected to emerge: this is, after all, a women's movement and men generally acknowledge that. They are learning to adapt to the demands of the women in their lives, case by case, rather than as some kind of mass movement. At home and at work, with individual partners and colleagues, they are negotiating the complex process of redefining gender roles and responsibilities. But they are not organised; there are no slogans; there are no signs of a counter-revolution.

Certainly, there are signs of a male backlash in particular cases. Some men have taken refuge in extreme and grotesque chauvinism and deliberately insensitive behaviour. Some men believe they have given away too much in the redistribution of power with women. Yet, underneath the widespread resentment, there is almost universal acceptance by men that this is a revolution which had to happen; that equality between the sexes is fundamental to a civilised and just society; that Australian women have had a lot of ground to make up.

Australian men might be confused and disorientated as they adapt to a significant shift in gender roles, but there is no evidence that they are crippled by this process. Far from being bruised and beaten under the impact of feminism, men are generally taking its arguments seriously and, even when they are slow to respond, they still recognise that they are caught in the midst of an inexorable process of social and cultural change. They typically report that they are 'coping reasonably well' with the changes they are being forced to make. Even those men who insist that they are not going to 'give up' without a struggle are conceding, by implication, that they *are* going to give up – at least in the sense of acknowledging that equality between the sexes is an incontrovertible fact of contemporary life.

Of course, the attitudes of Boomer males are changing more slowly than their behaviour: they learn what to *do* to please women much more quickly than they learn how to think or feel. But this is the way significant cultural change normally happens: changes in attitude tend to follow changes in behaviour. While the idea of a 'men's movement' as a kind of counter-revolution turns out to be largely mythical, so too does the idea that Boomer men have been so cowed by feminism that they retreated into an uncommunicative silence, even resisting intimacy with other men. On the contrary, there appears to be a very high level of openness and frankness between men when they are discussing gender issues.

The criticism often levelled at men by women – that they are reluctant to express their feelings – appears to be more a criticism of style than substance. In fact, men do not appear to be reluctant to express their feelings, but they might well choose to express them differently from the way those same feelings might be expressed by women. One of the healthiest signs of Boomer males' capacity to cope with the impact of the women's movement is the fact that they are now beginning to object, quite explicitly, to the idea that they should adapt to women's ways of thinking and expressing themselves. One of the meanings of their proposition that 'women *are* different' is that men should be free to acknowledge and even celebrate their own differences (whether biological or cultural) from women:

> *We are probably having more trouble than women, adapting to the changes, because women want us to act more like them. A woman comes to work on a shift and she expects the blokes' language to change because she's there. My wife wants to have her own car and her independence, but then she tells me the oil*

light has been on for weeks – she could check the dipstick just as easily as I can.

Men and women are different and they are interested in different things. Why not admit it? We'd all get along better if we didn't try to pretend that men should try and think like women . . . or vice versa.

'Why can't you show your emotions?' That's a favourite. They mean 'Why can't you act like a woman?' Why should we? If I felt like crying, I would. But I don't feel like crying as often as she does . . . and she doesn't feel like sex as often as I do. So there you go.

On balance, though, Boomer men are feeling pretty pleased with themselves over their response to the women's movement and their willingness to accept women's right to rethink the whole question of gender roles and responsibilities. But if there is one thing that riles men and causes them to think that 'the pendulum of gender justice may have swung too far', it is Affirmative Action in favour of women in the workplace. Even the men who acknowledge that Affirmative Action might have been necessary as a kick-start to the process of equalising opportunities for women at work are now inclined to think that it has run its course. The growing view among men is that Affirmative Action amounts, in practice, to a kind of 'reverse discrimination' which does not even serve the interests of women themselves, since they have to live with the perpetual question-mark about whether they have been appointed or promoted on the basis of merit, or on the basis of gender.

Culturally, the objection to Affirmative Action is also that it seems to encourage an anti-male prejudice which shows up in the sort of advertising that ridicules men, in draconian objections to light-hearted sexist remarks made by men about women (but not by women about men), and in a general sense that in any conflict between men and women, men are likely to be in the wrong (whether the conflict is expressed as competition for promotion, or a dispute over property or custody in the Family Court).

Nevertheless, men acknowledge that a revolution was overdue; that Australia had been something of a 'man's world'; that on any definition of equality, it was time for a more equitable sharing of power and responsibility between men and women:

> *I don't want my wife to be at home vacuuming. I think you should do everything together. The housework, looking after the children, everything. We have moved from defined, separate roles to merged roles.*
>
> *There was no negotiation about this kind of thing as far as my parents were concerned: what my father said was law and if my mother wanted to do something that he would disapprove of, she just had to go ahead and do it without telling him. But my wife and I consult with each other about everything. I couldn't go to Myer's and buy something for the house without consulting her.*

Yet men still have an uneasy sense that the 'whole sensitivity thing' might have gone too far, driven by the broader political correctness movement:

> *Men are probably having more trouble than women adapting to the changes. Several friends of mine who have gone into* de facto *relationships say that for the first couple of months, the woman was happy to fill the traditional role and then it didn't happen any more. It's a bit of a shock. Consciously or unconsciously, men expect their wives to be like their mothers.*

> *You have to be politically correct in pretty much everything you say, especially when it comes to gender issues. Everyone is terrified of treading on someone's toes in case you're torn down as a bigot. We think we're SNAGs and women turn around and say we're CHOPs [Chauvinistic Over-opinionated Pricks].*

THE FEMALE FOCUS: WINNING 'CHOICE'

When Boomer women tell their side of the story, they confirm many of the views expressed by men. Women do feel liberated;

women do feel more powerful than their mothers (and in many cases, than their husbands); women do feel as if they are well on the way to setting their own agenda; women do believe that their lives are more stimulating and interesting – though possibly less contented – than the lives led by their own mothers.

Boomer women revel in their liberation from 'house arrest' and appreciate the fact that, compared with their mothers, they are generally better educated and have more freedom to choose the kind of lives they will live:

> I would hate to have been a woman in my mother's generation, stuck at home all the time. Did your mothers ever go out? Mine never did. My parents used to have slide nights at our house but they never went out for dinner or had drinks with friends. We have a much better social life than my parents had, partly because we've got more money and partly because we have a different view of the world.

Women who combine paid employment with motherhood and housekeeping frequently complain about the stress involved (and often wonder about the effect on their children of the scarcity of time available for active parenting), but generally believe that their lives are more satisfying and stimulating than the lives of those who are full-time mothers and housekeepers.

Some full-time mothers agree: they report that they are weighed down by the relentlessness and the tedium of domesticity and that they can't wait to be relieved of the incessant burden of child care. But others see it quite differently: they revel in the opportunity to devote full attention and energy to running the household and supporting their children, while having time for proper recreation and the pursuit of other interests outside the home.

In most cases, though, Boomer women are quite explicit about the fact that they have far more choice about the direction and content of their lives than their mothers ever did. Indeed, as the women's liberation movement matures, there are growing signs of women being prepared to accept that there is more than one way of being 'liberated' and that paid employment is *not* the essential and only badge of feminism.

Boomer women know that the midlife crisis is more of a problem for men than it is for them; their male partners (or ex-partners) are more often gripped by insecurity and uncertainty than they are. Although many Boomer women are still struggling to reconcile the multiplicity of roles they are trying to play, at least they are clear about what those roles are. They acknowledge that the fundamental problem for men is that their traditional roles have been challenged without a new definition of masculinity having emerged.

Part of the fallout of this discrepancy between the clarity of women and the confusion of men is that Boomer women sometimes become impatient and unsympathetic as a result of living with a man who is suffering an identity crisis. It is increasingly common for Boomer women to think that men have lost their way and, while some of them decide to take charge and 'snap him out of it', others simply lose interest:

> *I'm turning things around in our house, with much difficulty. We are teaching our kids that we are both breadwinning, so everyone does everything. We are working towards teaching different role models from our parents' generation, but it isn't easy. I find I'm making more of the decisions . . . I suppose it's partly because he is having to adjust to the fact that I am away from the home a lot more than I used to be, and I am expecting him to take more responsibility with the children.*

For Boomer women – especially married women with children – paid employment has intensely symbolic significance: it carries the message that this is a woman who has found her own identity and, by adding paid employment to her other roles, is demonstrating that she is determined to 'have it all'.

Paid work, for Boomer women, is typically one contributor to a total sense of identity. For men, by contrast, the job itself has traditionally made the dominant contribution to a man's sense of identity. A man's job symbolised breadwinner status, with implications of duty and responsibility; for women (with the obvious exception of sole parents), the job is likely to be a symbol of *freedom* rather than responsibility.

When it comes to the bedroom, working mothers speak of their struggle against fatigue and the negative consequences of this for their sex lives. On the other hand, women with paid employment *do* report that they generally feel more liberated than their stay-at-home sisters and that this sense of liberation extends to a new-found freedom to take more initiatives in sexual activity or to say no to sex when they don't feel like it. This is one of the many paradoxes for the working wife and mother: she often feels stimulated and energised in ways which she is keen to express through her sexuality but, at the same time, she is often exhausted by the extra-ordinary physical demands made on her by the pace and complexity of her life.

At the heart of tensions between men and women lies the fundamental question of *power*. Women believe that the gender revolution has delivered what it promised them: a sense of being more powerful than their mothers ever dreamed of being. For them, that power expresses itself primarily in *choice* (rather than in the exercise of particular authority in a workplace). At the same time, men frequently report that they are becoming less powerful. The most successful partnerships are those which transcend the power struggle entirely and reach a point where concern with the whole question of gender roles – and the need to negotiate the apportionment of responsibilities – has diminished.

In *Fear of Fifty*, Erica Jong offers her own interpretation of the likely outcome of this power struggle:

I wanted men sexually but I did not want them to have *power* over me. This was something that men could not accept. Most men like power better than they like sex, and if you give them one without the other, they eventually rebel.[12]

As Boomer women reach their middle years, the meaning of 'choice' is changing. Many of these women will admit that, in the early flush of feminist enthusiasm, their vaunted freedom to choose actually felt like enslavement to the principle that a mother *must* have paid employment outside the home, in order not only to confirm her independent identity but also to equip her with the wherewithal to leave a marriage if she found it unsatisfactory. This is the first generation in which women have initiated the majority of divorces, so the need for financial independence was obvious: those women who have divorced their husbands will typically say that it was the job which provided the essential platform for their financial independence. Many of them, looking back on their parents' marriages, believe their mothers would have been happier had they been free to leave their fathers, but financial dependency was the sole restraining factor.

But a rethink is certainly under way. Younger Boomers are less inclined than their older sisters to assume that a 'liberated' woman must necessarily have paid employment. As the gender revolution matures, Boomer women are prepared to express regret that they tried to do too much, too soon, and all at once. Diana Bagnall, writing in the *Bulletin*, spoke for many of her generation when she said:

We who have had children in the past 10–15 years – myself included – have collaborated when we should have revolted. We have willingly offered our child-raising experience for experiment, suppressing our doubts about institutional care because to air them would be to accept fewer choices in our lives. And to step out of line.

We told only our closest friends about how awful the creche seemed when we first visited; about how the pain of separation from our child did not ease for months and sometimes never disappeared; about how we would give anything for a different life, a life where our child's infancy was not taken from us.

But we kept working, beating the same old drum. We should have shaken the walls of the corporations instead of climbing the ladders. We should have negotiated more parental leave, more flexible working hours, more part-time work – the humane solutions which social policy analysts and ordinary men and women have talked about for years and years.

But we are trapped – by a shrinking labour market, by the rising cost of living and by our political history. We mistrusted our feelings. In our haste to remake the world, we wiped the floor with motherhood. And now that we are sorry, we must be brave enough to say so.[13]

Diana Bagnall's point – echoed by growing numbers of Boomer women – is that 'equal rights' does not mean that all of those rights have to be exercised at once. 'Freedom of choice' does not mean that all options have to be embraced at the same time. For many women, the phrase 'have-it-all' has come to sound like a crushing burden rather than the threshold to a richer and more satisfying life.

To further complicate the issue, Boomer women are now hearing their teenage daughters criticising them for living life at too fast a pace:

My mother says that her mother was like a doormat to her father and the family, but I think my own mother is a doormat, too. She tries to cram too much in and it doesn't seem to be making her happy. I'm going to have it all, too, but I'm not going to try to have it all at once. When I have kids, I'm going to take a bit of time out to be a mother.

Whether economic imperatives will make it possible for those daughters to take the time out of the paid workforce to invest in motherhood remains to be seen. The Australian Institute of Family Studies has calculated that in 1995 a family had to earn 1.6 times the salary earned in 1970 to maintain the same standard of living and housing. That extra margin of income is generally earned by the mother, and it comes at a cost. Part of that cost is that someone else must care for the children.

But the daughters' reaction to the intensity of Boomer mothers' determination to be 'liberated' has caused many of the mothers to themselves embark on a painful rethink. When men say that they are still not sure that women know what they want out of the women's movement, there is at least some support for that view from the women themselves.

But doubts and reappraisals cannot dim the excitement which Boomer women still feel about their pioneering role:

> *I never knew it would be this hard, but there's no way I'd want to turn the clock back. I love my life, even though I wish I had more time, and more energy to cope with it properly. I know the kids have suffered in some ways but, on the other hand, they've got a more interesting mother than they would otherwise have had. And even my husband now admits that he finds me a more stimulating partner than I used to be. I still think that he is threatened by me sometimes, but we are working that out. This is a new world, and I am very glad to be part of it. If nothing else, my daughter knows, for sure, that she is free to choose from lots of different options. My mother never sent me that message, and it was pretty scary making it up as I went along.*

SAYING 'NO' TO RELIGION

The Boomers might turn out to have been the last generation of Australians to attend Christian Sunday Schools in large numbers. Certainly, they are the generation who have created something of a free-fall in church attendance. During the adult lives of the Boomers, the proportion of Australians attending church once a month or more often has fallen from 35 per cent to 20 per cent.

Of course, many Boomers are passionate about their religious observance, including those who have shifted their religious focus away from Christianity to other religions, especially Eastern religions like Buddhism.

But the major drift has been away from involvement in the kind of religious observance associated with the mainstream churches and their practise of conventional religion.

Considering the formative influences upon the Boomers, it is not surprising that religious faith has been eroded: this is the generation who grew up in the years when it seemed safe to jettison their parents' traditional moral values – including values rooted in religious faith – in favour of hedonism, materialism, consumerism and cynicism.

Now, in their middle years, many Boomers are ready to acknowledge that they have been hooked on materialism. Part of their generational midlife crisis arises from a growing sense that, when it comes to spirituality, they might have missed out:

> *Our homes are twice the size of the homes our parents had and we seem to have more of everything: cars, appliances . . . I have talked to my mum about this and she actually agrees with me that we have got it harder, even though we have got more in a material sense. Our parents were more contented and I think they enjoyed their children more. Our problem is that our material standards are so high, we want everything to be just perfect – including our kids.*

> *My parents' life was simpler. There is more financial pressure on us to keep up . . . perhaps it is natural to want a better standard of living than your parents had. Personally, I could think of nothing better than washing a plate in a sandy creek and drying it on the bank, and sleeping in a sleeping bag in a tent. I'd really like to spend more time in the bush, living the simple life. But my wife couldn't do without the microwave and the dishwasher. To be frank, I don't think any of us really would want to give up the material things which make life so comfortable. And yet . . .*

The question of whether Boomers would want to turn back the clock to a less prosperous but more 'contented' era is purely hypothetical: materialism has won the day and they continue to look to their possessions to provide them with the sense of security for which they yearn. Even those who have been driven to the reluctant conclusion that 'money can't buy happiness' still hope that if peace of mind eludes them, material comfort will offer some compensation, at least.

The Lucky Generation thought that 'solid values' came from a stable family life, supported by a steady income from a reliable supply of work. Looking at the restlessness of their offspring, they now wonder whether the high standard of living they offered their children has been directly responsible for *falling* standards in morality, values, and the related sense of being part of a stable community.

Hitting their middle years, some of the more thoughtful Boomers are tentatively approaching the same conclusion. But even when they finally get to the point of questioning whether materialism is a suitable framework for a system of personal and family values, Boomers find it difficult to contemplate any significant retreat from their present standard of material affluence. In particular, they find it hard to imagine living an acceptable life if they were to depart from the norm of the two-income family. Some of them take the plunge, however, and live to tell the tale:

> I know we are off the pace, but my wife reckons she would rather spend these precious years with the kids than get on the economic treadmill. She is going back to work when the children are out of primary school. Of course, the kids grizzle all the time because we can't afford to get them all the things that the other kids have. They don't realise that they are getting their mother's time – and that's something the other kids can't have. People who earn two incomes have to work very hard to extract pleasure from the money they earn. They have to pay people to do the things they can't do. They need more money to buy the clothes they have to wear to work, and the takeaway meals . . . you make sacrifices, one way or the other.

But such tentative retreats from the materialist ethic hardly amount to religious conversion. This is a generation which has taken some pride in their resistance to organised religion. Whether because religious sensitivities have been dulled by materialism, or because their early experiences of religion were a turn-off, or because their education (both formal and cultural) has made them more sceptical – for whatever reason, Boomers have typically substituted other passions for more traditional religious experience.

Being born in the middle of the 20th century, Boomers' education and outlook have been strongly influenced by the towering presence of two revolutionary figures: Freud and Einstein. Despite many Boomers not having formally studied or even been aware of the work of either of these men, the Freudian and Einsteinian views of the world have been deeply embedded in the culture which has shaped their generation.

Freud and Einstein, from their utterly different perspectives, have influenced Western popular culture by generating two powerful beliefs: the belief that all the answers to our psychological (and even spiritual) questions are within us; and the belief that *everything* (not just time and space, but knowledge and morality as well) is relative.

Every educated Boomer can tell you that $e=mc^2$. Every educated Boomer talks freely and confidently about 'the unconscious', 'repression', and the 'anal character' (terms unknown before Freud). Many, perhaps most, might not be able to explain Einstein's magic formula, nor Freud's central concepts, but their ideas have permeated Boomer culture. This combination of *subjectivity* and *relativity* represented a lethal challenge to earlier value systems based on a theistic spirituality and a set of moral absolutes.

With such intellectual influences as these running in tandem with rampant materialism, old-time religion did not stand much of a chance. But perhaps the yearnings generally identified as 'religious' are almost universal, so perhaps this generation has had to look to other 'gods' to satisfy its religious urge in a secular context. Plenty of possibilities have emerged: sex, travel, food, information and 'personal growth' are five strong contenders for deification, at least among middle-class Boomers (and most Boomers, having grown up in the heyday of egalitarianism, *feel* middle class).

Sex

All generalisations are dangerous because of the range of individual differences and the number of exceptions to every general assertion. But, as a generation, Boomers inherited their parents' belief that sex should be reserved for the person you are in love with; the difference was that they found it easy to justify a number of sexual partners by falling in love in the nick of time. 'I've never slept with anyone that I wasn't in love with' is a fairly typical Boomer claim – a claim which appals many of their parents with its rather transparent reinterpretation of their parents' morality.

Boomers seem to operate on the assumption that they *need* sex more than their parents did (or perhaps that they are more attuned to their own libido): they believe that the sexual content of contemporary culture has become so explicit and so intense that it has tuned them up to a point where sexiness is now regarded as a virtue. (On the other hand, Boomers show signs of disapproving of the inclination of their children's generation to regard sex as a form of physical recreation, with or without love.)

Sex with love has a quasi-religious significance for Boomers. They can talk about being 'close to God' at the moment of orgasm, and still keep a straight face. They can discern a spiritual dimension in the most carnal of experiences. They can speak about the liberation involved in sexual permissiveness, as if it is a liberation of the soul as well as the body. Boomers worship sex and sexiness in a way which has shocked their parents and appals some of their children. Impatient to pair off at an early age, they have been obsessed with pairing off (either in fact or in fantasy) ever since.

Travel

The Lucky Generation discovered the joys of travel in the 1950s and 1960s, and embarked on such undertakings as the 'Women's Weekly Discovery Tour' aboard ocean liners before the Boeing 747 revolutionised tourism by air.

Baby Boomers are inveterate travellers, but as their travels become more exotic, they want you to know that they are not simply rubbernecking foreign climes: they are discovering themselves through cross-cultural experience (whether that takes the form of exploring their cultural roots, or exposing themselves to the emotional and physical challenge of the Third World).

Boomers have created yet another boom: the boom in 'significant' holidays, which might range from the 'primitive chic' (to borrow a phrase from Walter Truett Anderson)[14] of a Himalayan trek or an African safari, to educational and self-improving holidays offering the experience of authentic American gospel-singing or an educational exposure to European culture.

Plenty of Boomers still take holidays for the purpose of relaxation and leisure, but the quasi-religious holiday experience is increasingly popular among those who can afford it. Boomers who feel unfulfilled by lives destabilised by uncertainty and insecurity often look to a holiday experience for a brush with longed-for perfection in one form or another – the perfection of simplicity, of sophistication, of discipline, of exploration – but, always, of heightened self-awareness.

Food

Boomers mock their parents' lack of sophistication when it comes to food, regarding themselves as the great beneficiaries of gastronomic multiculturalism. They are proud of their exposure to a wide range of 'ethnic' foods and of their understanding of ingredients which were, literally, foreign to their parents. Boomers who have chosen to deify food are not so much health-conscious as trend-conscious. Particularly in Sydney and Melbourne, leading-edge restaurants acquire the status of shrines for pilgrims who have located their souls in their stomachs. For them, one of the most 'religious' of rituals is being seen at the latest shrine where a protracted discussion about the menu will soon reveal the true believers and expose apostasy.

Coffee, in particular, has become heavily symbolic. Boomers have presided over the retreat from their parents' reverence for tea; today, coffee is undisputed monarch of the hot drink market. But, for leading-edge Boomers, it's not just coffee (or 'a coffee', as they have taken to saying): the degree of their enlightenment is revealed by the expression of subtle preferences (between, say, cafe latte and flat white) and a confident ability to order the variety of coffee that is just right for each occasion: cappuccino, long black, short black, double espresso, black with milk on the side, to say nothing of particular beans and blends.

Information

Boomers will never catch up with their children when it comes to the mastery of information technology, but many of them have been sufficiently dazzled by the information revolution to fall for the trap of believing that information is a new kind of god; that information will somehow 'save' them; that having more information is bound to be better than having less.

Rather like religious pilgrims of old, who couldn't get enough piety, the pilgrims on the information superhighway usually turn out to be info-gluttons. Many bewildered Boomers are to be found among their number, trudging obediently and hopefully towards the bright light of Knowledge, or even Wisdom.

Information has become the symbol of the new materialism, and Boomers are no strangers to the comforting idea that more is better and, accordingly, that possession is a suitable goal. So they consume information as voraciously as they have previously consumed Thai food, experiential holidays, sexual partners or cars.

'Personal growth'

The personal growth movement of the 1970s was tailor-made for Boomers who were getting the first inkling that their future was not going to be plain sailing and that they might need some personal resources beyond the material. Though many Boomers were too young to be fully-fledged hippies in the 1960s, they learned from their older brothers and sisters all about encounter groups and the various pathways to the goal of 'liberation'.

Some manifestations of the personal growth movement gave them a respectable way of dropping out, without the beads (but, possibly, with the marijuana). That movement perfectly matched the emerging Boomer philosophy of 'Look after Number One' and

'Do your own thing': it appeared to offer a conceptual or even intellectual framework for an ethical system devoid of the notion of restraint, or the practice of self-denial. Though it was not always recognised as an antisocial movement which carried the potential to destroy relationships, it often turned out in practice to feed self-centredness and to enshrine the idea that personal growth was the way to nirvana (where 'personal growth' often meant not much more than 'feeling good').

Part of the folklore of the movement was that 'if only one of you grows, you are likely to grow apart', and that was what planted the seeds of destruction in many marriages and other relationships. One partner departed for a weekend retreat to 'find themselves' and then discovered they had embarked on a far longer journey than the other partner had bargained for or was prepared to entertain. Spouses announced that they had developed such a heightened awareness of themselves and their potential that they felt constrained and constricted by being married to an ungrown and unaware partner. 'Awareness' became a quasi-religious term.

Many people undoubtedly benefited from the therapeutic effects of personal-growth courses, seminars, workshops and encounter groups. Many others discovered that awareness was just another false god, promising bliss but delivering frustration or dis-illusionment.

Whether the Boomers' new gods were located in a rumpus-room extension, sexual experimentation, an encounter with the exotic, a flickering screenful of data or the illusion of mind expansion, this generation has turned out to be no less interested in religious experience than any other generation; the difference is that, in large numbers, they rejected their parents' and grandparents' religion in favour of quasi-religious pursuits and practices of their own.

In trying to fill the vacuum created by their rejection of the Christian faith of their parents' generation (however nominal or perfunctory its practice), Boomers have flirted with many alternatives. Some have explored Eastern religions, where they might find it easier to believe in reincarnation than resurrection; others have engaged in faddish flirtations with ancient forms of mysticism and 'spiritual' therapy such as clairvoyance, aromatherapy, crystals, yoga, meditation (with or without mantras), or Scientology. Every conceivable pathway to peace of mind has had its appeal to a generation who, having prided themselves on their iconoclasm, are still looking for replacement icons of their own.

As it dawns on Boomers that they are going to live to a ripe old age, but that the turbulence of their lives is unlikely to subside, their earlier spirit of recklessness is giving way to an inevitable engagement with the idea of mortality and how to keep it at bay. The obsession with health and fitness is, for many Boomers, a belated acknowledgement that 'we might be here for a long time *as well as* a good time'. The upper price limit on joggers has yet to be reached, as Boomers jog for their lives and, like religious zealots of old, seek enlightenment through intense self-discipline sometimes amounting almost to self-flagellation. (Who said the Boomers were saying 'no' to religion?)

THE EMOTIONAL HAZARDS OF OVER-PARENTING

Because Boomers are so confident that they have been better parents than their own parents were, and because they are proud of the closeness they feel exists between them and their children, they are particularly sensitive to any signs in their children's behaviour which might imply good (or bad) parenting. Parents are always proud of their children's charming qualities and their achievements, of course, and they tend to empathise with their children's disappointments and failures. But for Boomers, even more than for their own parents, children have become a reflection of their 'success' as parents. Indeed, many Boomer parents would be happy to be judged by their children's feats.

Such a sentiment sounds, at first, like an echo of the mothers of the Lucky Generation who, in defending their role as full-time parents, claim that they are happy to assess the value of their own lives in terms of 'how we feel about our families – how our children have turned out'. In fact, quite different motivations are at work in the two generations.

Lucky Generation mothers speak of their *devotion to motherhood* and make the confident assertion that they gave their children full-time attention. Boomers, by contrast, are feeling distinctly uneasy about whether they have devoted enough time to parenting, especially to mothering, and so they are looking, rather more anxiously, for the reassuring signs in their children that they have indeed been good parents.

The trouble is that, as for all parents before them, Boomers are finding that the signs are actually ambiguous. Some Boomers are now beginning to wonder whether they might have tried too hard and, in the process, been too permissive, too indulgent and too generous (in a materialistic sense) to their children. In wanting to achieve that classic Boomer goal – *staying close* – they fear that, rather than simply closing the generation gap, they might have compromised their own position as parents. They wonder whether they should have given their children the advantage of tougher discipline, stronger leadership, or even the reassurance of a clearer distinction between the positions of parent and child:

I can feel myself doing it, but I can't help it . . . I just want the kids to have the best of everything, even though it wasn't like that for me. I remember getting my first pair of jeans when I was in Grade 10. Now they get jeans when they're three or four.

I'll tell you a thing that gets to me . . . everyone seems to think that all the kids have to have a room of their own. Why? When I was little, I slept with my brother in a big bed . . . then we graduated to double bunks. We never thought about having a room of our own, but it has become the big thing. Kids expect it.

Comments like these indicate that some Boomer parents are pre-pared to see their overzealous parenting as a shortcoming, and yet they find it hard to resist the pressure to keep indulging their child-ren and to strive for 'peace at any price'.

There is no mystery about these conflicting attitudes. Boomer parents believe that they are so stressed, and so exhausted by their stress, that their rather soft attitude to their children is an auto-matic response. They know they are *compensating*.

But even that is not the whole story. Boomers' parenting is, for many of them, an opportunity to recapture the promise of their own childhood, that this generation would be as lucky as their par-ents had been.

So the compensatory aspect of indulgent parenting is two-edged: it is an attempt to mask the insecurities of parents who, though they have tried so hard, wonder whether they have put enough time, devotion and well-directed effort into parenting; and it is a way of compensating for their own disappointments:

My daughter didn't really want everything, but we've given her everything and she's accepted it.

We've taken our children overseas a number of times and what worries me is, what will be a big deal for your children to achieve? Even in material things? For us, overseas travel was a big deal and something you tried to achieve when you finished university. But what is there for our kids when everything is so available . . . doesn't it take some of the awe out of life?

I sometimes wonder whether we are so busy giving our kids everything that we have forgotten that we had to wait for a lot of these things ourselves. You think everything was rosy back in the fifties and sixties, but I think our childhoods were reason-ably unspoiled. We had a lot more freedom and a lot less pres-sure . . . and we didn't have the same kind of crazy expectations that our kids have. Look at toys . . . who would have dreamed of asking for something as expensive as a Nintendo, or some of

this new computer software. A bike was the big thing . . . some
kids these days are on to their second or third bikes.

The Boomers' parents suspect that they might have over-indulged their offspring in response to an economic context which seemed to promise prosperity for all. But the Boomers themselves recall childhoods which were positively disciplined and restrained, compared with those they are furnishing for their own children. Boomers obviously don't speak about deprivation or hardship when they reflect on their childhood (since they were not, after all, the children of a Depression or a World War), but they certainly use words like 'discipline', 'simplicity' and 'respect' when they try to convey an impression about their lives as children. The Lucky Generation might feel that they failed to convey their non-material values to their Boomer offspring with sufficient clarity, but the Boomers recall childhoods which were, indeed, strongly influenced by their parents' moral frameworks.

Wherever the truth might lie, Boomers are convinced that they had more respect for their parents than they are receiving from their own children. As they hit their middle years, Boomers are beginning to wonder whether the notion of children's rights has got out of hand, whether children are becoming unacceptably assertive, and whether the very concept of discipline has irretrievably faded.

As in so many other examples of human experience, Boomers' attitudes towards their children's generation are shot through with contradictions. On the one hand, they are proud of how seriously they have taken parenting and of how close they have managed to stay to their own children; on the other hand, they report being appalled by the assertiveness, materialism or sheer rudeness of today's youngsters. While believing that they have been better parents than their own parents were, they give their parents credit for having 'run the family' in ways which they themselves seem not prepared to do. While criticising their own parents for having been rather dull or conventional or tunnel-visioned, they admire them for having created a positive childhood experience for the Boomers.

Such a thicket of paradoxes is impenetrable. But it is clear that

Boomers wish that they might have been able to blend some of their own emphasis on permissiveness with a little more of their parents' emphasis on discipline:

> *Kids these days are ruder, less disciplined and they expect the best of everything. It comes from kids being able to say disgusting things to their parents and get away with it. My mother is quite open-minded, but she admits my children are much harder to discipline than we were. We are all told we must not physically discipline them . . . kids regard themselves as being far more adult than we ever were, and they insist on having their say. When I was a child, dinner was at six o'clock and you only opened your mouth to shovel food in. Now, if my husband wants to watch the seven o'clock news on TV, the kids get upset because they want to watch 'Neighbours'. If my father didn't like something we were watching on TV, he would turn it off and you wouldn't dream of turning it back on again. But now it's all a matter of discussion and negotiation . . . there's more input from the children.*

> *The kids' language appals me, but what can you do? They get it off the TV and they think that is the way to talk. You would be correcting them every five minutes if you wanted to change them. It really disgusts me when I hear young people on the train . . . it is all fucking this, and fucking that.*

Boomers are torn on the subject of discipline. As a generation, they remain convinced that corporal punishment is evil, yet they hanker after the idea that it did them no harm and might, in certain cases, have done their own kids a power of good. Part of the problem, as they now see it, is that children themselves know that corporal punishment has been discouraged or even outlawed and, if they want to be cheeky or disrespectful, the worst that can happen is the descent into an angry war of words. Boomers, who saw themselves as a most confident generation of young people, are now unnerved by the swaggering overconfidence they see in their children's generation (if not in their own children):

> We got the strap at home and at school, and it didn't do us any harm. We learned how to behave pretty quickly. We weren't allowed to answer back, that's for sure. Now my kids say 'shut up' to me . . . I suppose it is all in the tone of voice . . . they are not really being abusive.

> I remember once asking how old my grandmother was and what her Christian name was, and I got into trouble. I suppose we were taught to respect our elders more, back then.

As it begins to dawn on the Boomers that, in spite of all their wishes to the contrary, there might be a new generation gap opening up between them and their children, they even find themselves wondering whether the education system is to blame. Parents generally admire the rising level of their children's education and find it hard to criticise the idea that children should strive for anything less than the best possible education. And yet, in occasional private ruminations, they wonder whether over-education is a possibility – either because it turns children into 'smart arses' or because it generates unrealistic expectations about what life might be able to deliver them:

> Educationally, they have so many more opportunities than we had, but where do they lead? Where are the jobs going to come from? Are we simply educating them to do things that they won't be able to do? The higher they go with their education, the more they will find it difficult to get work. I hate to say it, but they are almost over-educated, some of them. There are more jobs for clerks than for rocket scientists, let's face it.

Nevertheless, Boomer parents are in awe of the quality and quantity of their children's education: they firmly believe that children have a more adventurous and challenging time at school and that the educational outcome is more sophisticated, more comprehensive and more advanced than it was for them:

> *They are encouraged to think more and express their opinions more . . . I would have freaked out at some of the things they have to do. I can help them with their homework up to a point, but even in the upper years of primary school, we were finding that some of the stuff was beyond us.*
>
> *Still, you have to ask where this is all heading. The pressure on kids to improve their education is incredible . . . you practically need the HSC to become a storeman. My son actually wanted to leave school at 16 . . . but there was no way. We could do that, but our kids can't. They have to stick it out.*

Reflecting on their children's schooling, Boomers also note another generational difference: they have found themselves turning up to school functions – educational, social, sporting – far more often than they can remember their own parents ever having done. They have crowded the sidelines at sporting events, egging their sons and daughters on – partly, it seems, to prove how involved they are as parents. (For some of them, reflections on their own parents' absence from school sport leads to the conclusion that their parents never felt the *need* to offer such structured support, since mothers, in particular, were full-time parents at home. 'Do we have more to prove than our parents did?' That's an issue which many Boomers find too tough to confront.)

Attitudes to their children's education reveal another strand of the 'perfection' ideal which often permeates Boomers' thinking. In ways which their own parents would find alarming and inappropriate, middle-class Boomers typically extended their desire to give their children 'the best' into the school and the classroom: the best possible school (whether public or private), the best possible teacher for *every* subject, the best possible coach for every sport – Boomers place more emphasis on the *quality* of teaching than their parents did, and are correspondingly willing to attach more blame to the school for shortcomings in everything from their children's exam marks to their manners.

Writing in the *Weekend Australian* on the subject of over-parenting, Deborah Hope quotes the case of a mother at a private girls' school in Sydney:

> *It's like being in the police. It is exhausting because you have to negotiate all the time and you have to watch them all the time. They are old enough to want autonomy, but they are not street-wise. They are much too protected. If they want to go to a party I have to ring up to check a parent will be home. Should they be allowed to go out to the movies at night in a group? As a parent, you just don't know how much independence you can allow.*[15]

The same article quotes the Director of Melbourne's Centre for Child and Family Development, Ruth Schmidt Neven, who remarks that in making certain our children are engaged in purposeful activity from the time they wake to the time they fall asleep at night, we may be robbing them inadvertently of a key prerequisite for real learning to take place: the capacity to be alone with their own thoughts. As Deborah Hope concludes: 'Aloneness is not a condition highly regarded in our society. Parents of the 1990s intrude on children's need to be left alone from the moment they are born.'

All that time new mothers spend gazing at their infants, cooing to them and holding them in their arms might actually be stifling their development, according to Deborah Jackson, author of *Do Not Disturb*: 'Our intensity does not liberate our children, it disturbs their natural growth . . . We sit gazing at them when they could be on the sidelines observing us.' Jackson says that babies enjoy the occasional kiss and tickle, but their real business is to witness the actions, interactions and surroundings of parents or carers and other children.[16]

This preoccupation with children as babies has tended to persist, for Boomer parents, into the adolescence and even the young adulthood of their offspring.

Ruth Schmidt Neven believes childhood is under threat because our consumer society presents parenting as a package able to produce the perfect child product. Anxious parents may believe, falsely, that the more they do for their children, the more successful they will be. 'But the most important resource parents can give their kids is their own relationship with them,' she says. 'Parents' presence is vital.'

Such views are both reassuring and frightening to Boomers who battle to find the time for parenting, while believing passionately in the importance of their relationships with their children. Often, their solution has been to over-organise their children's time so that they can schedule their own contacts with their offspring. Reflecting an emerging view in child psychology, Hope suggests that we might have to examine whether, in hurrying our children from activity to activity, 'we are indulging them or ourselves'.

These are largely middle-class and upper-middle-class concerns, of course. As Hope puts it: 'Parental indulgence is not an issue in depressed neighbourhoods.' She quotes a teacher at a school in Sydney's disadvantaged south-west who says he wishes he had more parents showing an interest in their children's welfare and offering more tangible support. Rather ruefully, he envies those middle-class schools where 'over-parenting' might become a problem.

Clinical psychologist Wendy Cohen similarly remarks that it is always preferable for children to have an involved parent rather than an ignoring or rejecting parent. To be 'unwanted and unloved' is the worst problem, she says. Cohen is therefore cautious about regarding over-parenting as a sign of indulgence when, in many cases, it is simply a sign of parental love and concern, and she attributes some of the increased earnestness of parents to sociological change in an environment of affluence:

We are having children later, and older parents place so much more concentration on the child. These days, a child is deprived if they are not up and running with the Internet at 10 years old. But we have to ask at what point is it indulgence, and at what point is it just societal change.[17]

One irony in all this is that at the very time when some commentators – and some Boomer parents themselves – are questioning whether Boomers are guilty of over-parenting, their own parents are inclined to criticise them for under-parenting.

Similarly, Steve Biddulph, author of *Manhood* and *Raising Boys*, is on record as saying that 'this is the most underfathered generation ever'[18] (just when Boomer fathers are making the proud claim to be more active parents than their own fathers were).

The gap between those two views seems to arise from disagreement over the relative importance of the *quantity* and *quality* of time spent with children. While the Boomers draw comfort from their reliance on the concept of 'quality time', their parents (and a number of authorities in the field of child care) suspect that the real job of parents is to 'be around' for their children, rather than engaging in too-carefully programmed contacts with them.

When Boomer parents look as dispassionately as they can at the quality of life with their children and then try to compare that with what they recall – however mistily or rose-tintedly – of life in their own family households, they readily identify two major differences between them and their kids.

First, they believe they have created households characterised by more *open communication* than existed when they were children. Their children get the good news and the bad news; they know all about their parents' highs and lows. If there is financial trouble, or if Dad is worried about being retrenched, the kids are in on the secret. If Mum has a new boyfriend, the kids will be the first to know (since honesty – defined as 'letting it all hang out' – is a very particular virtue the Boomers want to claim for themselves). Indeed, she'll probably consult them and seek their 'permission' to proceed with the new relationship, and then resent the power her children seem to have over her, or worry about the 'emotional burden' they are being asked to carry at a young age.

Boomers now wonder whether all this openness might have been unrestrained to the point of insensitivity to the emotional needs of their children. (They used to mock their own parents for being inhibited about such things, but now they wonder whether 'not in front of the children' had some moral point to it, after all.)

The second difference is that, for all kinds of reasons, Boomers perceive their children as having been *more selfish*, right from the beginning, than the Boomers themselves were. They can see that they might have played some part in this: they were the ones who encouraged their children to 'be themselves', and the education system repeatedly reinforced that same message. Now they wonder whether they might have indulged their children's wishes to a point which led the children to cling to that most fundamental belief of infancy – the belief that we are each at the centre of our own little universe:

> *My 19-year-old daughter is the most selfish creature that walked the earth. I can tell you it's not Harmony Cottage at our place. The age for doing everything is getting younger . . . she didn't really have much to look forward to in her late teens: she did it all when she was 13 or 14.*

> *Maybe we brought this on ourselves. We were so keen for our kids to have every opportunity and every little indulgence we could afford . . . we even kitted them out for sport as if they were mini-professionals. No wonder they got the idea that they were important. I don't think my parents ever let me get away with thinking that.*

Sexual values are a particular case in point: Boomers find themselves wondering whether contemporary teenagers are too ready to explore all options in matters of sex – as in other areas of life – without having reached the level of maturity necessary to cope with a sexual relationship:

> *They are going all the way younger than we did . . . but at least they are more open about it. My daughter was 15 when she slept with her boyfriend in our house. They are going to do it anyway, so you have to get used to it. Sometimes when she asks*

if so-and-so can sleep over, I stop and think, 'You can't have it all the time' . . .

When Boomers' conversation about 'the younger generation' turns dark, the subject of youth suicide inevitably comes up. They know it is their children's generation who have doubled the rate of youth male suicide (though the rate of *attempted* suicide seems to be about the same for young women as well). They know that many members of their children's generation are suffering from feelings of alienation and depression. They know that 'too many' young teenagers are sexually entangled before they have the emotional equipment to deal with it. They know that drugs are a much greater problem for their kids than they were for the Boomers themselves – even in the famously hallucinatory 1960s. They know that the bleak employment outlook for the rising generation must take its emotional toll, and they know that excessive materialism is likely to lead to excessive disillusionment. And, very quietly, they speculate about the role of broken families in the whole sad scenario:

Are they . . . you know . . . growing up too fast, maybe? Is it all happening to them before they are old enough to cope with it? Have we failed them?

TAKING STOCK

Leading-edge Boomers, born in the late 1940s and early 1950s, are now into their forties and early fifties. The nuclear holocaust has not happened and seems less likely to happen than it once did: they are still here, and so are their spouses, their ex-spouses, their kids and their debts.

How have they responded to the discovery that there is a future, after all, and that they will have to continue coping with it?

Being human, their response is another bundle of contradictions. They want to simplify their lives, but they seem to keep adding more activities, creating more challenges and acquiring more possessions to distract them from that nagging midlife question: Is this all there is?

They still spend, spend, spend, often claiming, even on a salary of $80 000 or more, that they can't make ends meet.

But having grown up with pride in their own recklessness – they saw themselves as iconoclasts, after all – they have now become obsessed with safety. They have even become keen on the idea of tougher regulations, including censorship, to curb other people's excesses. Airbags for their cars, security systems for their homes, radiation screens for their computers and mobile phones to keep track of their children – for a generation supposed to have been careless of the future, Boomers have become surprisingly interested in their own and other people's survival.

They are contradictory, too, about food: fast but healthy is how they want it, so they seek a balance between voracious consumption of what they affectionately call 'junk food' and the home cooking of carefully selected ingredients. Stir-fry is the perfect compromise for them (as *Impatiens* is the perfect plant for their gardens).

Indeed, Boomers' changing attitudes to diet and health are a good indication of the way in which their view of the world is changing. Through the frantic years of the 1980s, they were drawn to the proposition that health is the pathway to happiness. They embraced exercise programs and all kinds of faddish diets; they eschewed sugar, salt and red meat; they worried about dairy products; they constructed a protective fortress of bran around themselves each morning to insulate them from the ravages of the day; they strove for ever-lighter food.

As their stress levels continued to rise, though, they arrived at the beginning of the 1990s with a new outlook. Reflecting on their parents' simpler and happier lives, they began to wonder whether they themselves had got it all round the wrong way. Perhaps health wasn't the pathway to happiness, after all; perhaps happiness was the pathway to health. As support for that contrary proposition gathers momentum, Boomers are starting to look for some of the short cuts to happiness (since they are still, generationally, inclined to go for the quick solution).

So they are trying hard to relax about diet and even about exercise. They are encouraged to learn that walking might be just as beneficial to their fitness as jogging. They are pleased to hear that red meat is back on the 'approved' menu (though many of their teenage daughters are not yet convinced). They are beginning to reappraise the value of 'fast food' in more positive terms as they warm to the idea that it's not necessarily *what* you eat, but *how* you eat, that determines whether an eating occasion is healthy.

The picture of a stressed and harassed person wolfing down 'healthy' food now strikes them as being unhealthy. Conversely, the idea of the family laughing and chatting over a takeaway pizza, or even sitting around a table in a hamburger restaurant, seems inherently attractive and healthy. They want life to be simpler, and eating looks like a good place to start. So if the takeaway food or the restaurant fare is somewhat beyond their control in strictly nutritional terms, then there is the reassuring offset of a relaxed eating occasion to compensate.

Some trend-watchers have dubbed this the 'pleasure revenge', citing the growing evidence of Boomers abandoning the exercise machine for the massage table, as well as going for 'taste' rather than 'goodness' when a choice has to be made. (As a result, Boomers are likely to put on more weight: perhaps it will be the middle-age spread that will finally convince them of the passage of time.)

The working mothers of the baby-boom generation, certainly, are coming to the view that it is a sensible redeployment of their time to devote less of it to cooking and more of it to eating:

One thing the migrants have taught us is to enjoy eating more. Australians have always been such private eaters – such quiet eaters – but when you look at the Greeks and Italians . . . and even some of the Asians . . . you realise that eating can be a really pleasant family affair, and a social occasion. I think that is healthy. It's good to eat healthy food as well, but I think the main thing is to relax. I think we've all been a bit uptight about our diets.

And retirement? That still seems a long way off to the Boomers: 'We'll worry about that when the time comes.' Occasionally they experience a moment's panic as they realise that pensions might not be as readily available for them as they have been for the Lucky Generation, and so they look thoughtfully at their own children and wonder whether, when the time comes, the necessary support will be forthcoming. That's a thought upon which they are disinclined to dwell (though, according to Ross Gittins, Economics Editor of the *Sydney Morning Herald*, the combined effects of compulsory superannuation and increasing middle-class ownership of shares will ultimately cushion the retirement blow).[19]

The Boomers might have decided that as a prescription for a lifetime of happiness, *All you need is love, love, love* was a bit hollow and a bit simplistic. But they are still inclined to cling to another tenet of Beatles philosophy: *Let it be*. Their greatest source of tension is that they are stressed by the present, while still wanting to resist the future. As the generation raised on the high-octane fuel of one of Australia's most optimistic periods, they still aspire to live in the moment with as much intensity as possible. They were caught in the generational surge of the 1960s, and they hope that they might catch another wave. 'Let's give it a bit more time,' they are saying. 'Something might turn up . . . things usually work out for the best.' The expectations created for them by the boom years of the 1950s and 1960s might not have been fulfilled, and that's disappointing. But those expectations have not quite faded: the Boomers hope, as they always have, that they will ultimately inherit their birthright.

4
BORN IN THE 1970S: THE 'OPTIONS' GENERATION

A group of seven 19- and 20-year-old women are sitting in the living room of a house in suburban Sydney, chatting about their outlook on life, as part of a research project designed to explore the emerging attitudes and values of young Australians.

All of them have their hair in ponytails. All of them are dressed completely in black. Some are wearing long skirts, some pants; the tops vary in style, but they are all black. And all of them are wearing elastic-sided boots; some black, some tan.

They are talking about their reluctance to 'pair off' and their disgust at the discovery that one of their friends from high school has just announced that she is engaged to be married. They talk enthusiastically about their own freedom, their flexibility, and their determination to, as they say, 'hang loose'. Above all, they are talking about the enormous gap between their sense of the options which life offers them and what they see as the conformist behaviour of their parents' generation. That generation is, of course, the Boomers: the generation who felt *they* were breaking the mould and resisting entry into the tunnel of conformity through which their own parents had passed:

There's no way I want to be like my parents. I love them and everything, but I want to have a much better marriage than theirs, and I want to do heaps more things than they have done. And if I ever have children, there's no way I'm going to keep working full-time . . . I will take a few years off to be a proper mother.

I'd give much more commitment to my marriage than my parents have, even if it wasn't going to last a lifetime. But while I was in it, I'd want to be really committed to it. But I don't even want to think about it for another ten years. I want to run on my own for a while. I wouldn't have a family until I was content with myself.

My parents work too hard, anyway. It is just all grind, grind, grind. Duty is all very well, but I would want to have a bit more fun out of life than they have managed to get. I think one of the advantages of being better educated than our parents is that you develop a more balanced view of life. Better education mightn't guarantee you the job you want, but you have a better perspective on life. You are less driven, somehow . . .

The recurring theme is *individuality*. In spite of the conformity of their dress, their argot and their attitudes, they are strongly resistant to any suggestion that they are 'typical' or that they are a generation who can be pigeonholed. Towards the end of the discussion, one of the girls turns to the researcher, wagging her finger, and says: 'Don't you try to make any generalisations about us.' (I was the researcher in question, and I wouldn't have dared; not there and then, anyway.)

Across town, a group of young men in their early twenties are taking part in the same project. One of them is remarking – matter-of-factly, but with an edge of bitterness – that he has now applied unsuccessfully for 200 jobs. As a boost to his flagging self-esteem, he mentions that he was 'in the last five, twice'.

One of his friends comments that although he was intending to get into the building game and had started work as a brickie's labourer, he was now working in an instant printing shop and loving it. He ventured the opinion that 'as long as you are prepared to take what's going, there's work to be had', but this did not go down too well with his unemployed mate, who declared that he was willing to go anywhere and do anything.

A third member of the group was also unemployed, but appeared quite relaxed: 'I tried work once,' he said, 'but I didn't like it.' No one laughed; he was simply expressing what this generation holds to be true: that *all* options are open, and work is merely one of them.

In any case, work was not the main focus of the conversation; the main focus was on having a good time. This was a group of friends who valued each other's company, respected each other's points of view and spent most of their spare time together:

> *We hang out in parks, and we drink. We go camping, and we get smashed. We go swimming, and we get smashed. We go to the drive-in, and we get smashed. We go fishing, and we get smashed . . . Being with each other and not doing anything that you have to do is fun. We go to the pub, talk about cars, and get pissed. We are getting smashed basically nearly every night. In fact, I know some people who have been drunk every night since New Year, and we're into March already.*
>
> *All the girls look better after a few beers. That's when you get the guts to go up and talk to them . . . when you've had a few. I get dragged along to some really awful nightclubs. I usually drink until I don't feel totally stupid about dancing, then I dance.*

> *What's the reason to hurry? There's no rush about finding the right job, or the right girl. We've got plenty of time. I'm not going to be like my old man and settle down at twenty-five with three kids and a mortgage. That sort of thing locks you in for life. Can you imagine it? The girls we're going out with now . . . it's really just for the sex.*

Life, thus far, has taught the generation born in the 1970s to keep their options open; to wait and see what will happen next; to postpone long-term commitments in favour of short-term goals and temporary solutions.

And why not? This is the generation born into one of the most dramatic periods of social, cultural, economic and technological development in Australia's history: the age of discontinuity, the age of redefinition, the age of uncertainty – call it what you will. They don't share their parents' or grandparents' conscious anxiety about the rapid rate of change and its destabilising effect on society: for them, constant change is the air they breathe; the water they swim in. It is simply the way the world is.

This is the generation for whom the women's movement was already 'history' by the time they hit puberty; the generation who take equality between the sexes for granted, though they have a clear sense of the differences between men and women. It is the generation who know that women can do anything they choose: they know that more than 50 per cent of university students and 45 per cent of the workforce are female. (In the 20–24 age group, female graduates now outnumber males.)

Most of their mothers have paid employment outside the home. This is not regarded as a big deal, or even worth mentioning. Those who are still at school don't expect Mum to be there making afternoon tea for them when they get home, and they vaguely wonder why she even bothers mentioning the fact that that's what her own mother used to do.

On the other hand, roughly 750 000 Australians under the age of 24 live in households where no one is currently earning any wages, so the reality of unemployment is pretty stark for the members of the Options Generation included in that figure. Even if their parents have work, about one-third of young job-seekers face the bleak prospect of a labour market that doesn't want them – at least, not yet.

To their parents and grandparents, the sharp rise in the divorce rate over the past 20 years seems cataclysmic, shaking the very foundations of the institution of marriage and the family. But to the rising generation, nothing has changed: from the time they became aware of the nature of marriage and divorce, they have known that lots of their friends live with one parent, so what's the big deal? The adolescents and young adults of the Options Generation don't bother to exchange information about their parents' marital status: the word 'family' has such diverse meanings for them, it is hardly worth discussing. This doesn't mean, of course, that they have all avoided the pain and anguish of their parents' divorces; in some cases, they carry emotional wounds which are reopened by every reminder of their parents' estrangement. But almost one million dependent children live with only one parent, so the Options Generation understands that when it comes to families – like everything else – people will exercise their options . . . and that's 'cool' for them.

It is in their lifetime that the proportion of births out of wedlock has risen from ten to 25 per cent. This is the generation who have grown up with the idea of multiculturalism, who generally assume it is inevitable that Australia will become a republic (though this is a subject of little interest to most of them), who have always been aware of AIDS, who know there is a drug culture in their school or suburb, and who know how to gain access to it if they want to. (The idea of someone becoming an *unwitting* victim of the drug culture seems laughable to them.)

This is the generation who have always known that the global environment is a precious resource which earlier generations have abused, and which must now be protected if the species is to survive. It is also, of course, the generation for whom the rate of male youth suicide has doubled, to the point where Australia now has one of the highest rates of youth suicide in the world.

This is our most highly educated and media-stimulated generation. For those who can cope with that, the world has become an exciting place; for those who have been overwhelmed by it, or who have dropped out without being noticed, the world is a bleak and forbidding place – this is also the generation who have given us 'street kids' in disturbingly large numbers.

They are a generation utterly adapted to the idea that today's technology will soon be superseded by something which is already appearing over the horizon. Things like e-mail, mobile phones, fax machines, personal computers, the Internet, interactive media and even 'virtual reality' are all rather ho-hum. Although the children of the 1970s are inclined to regard the generation coming after them as the real tech-heads and nerds, it was they who irritated their parents by being able to program a VCR without reading the manual.

Changes and developments in technology are, for them, simply another symptom of the kind of world in which they live: *everything* is changing; *everything* is relative; *everything* will have to adapt to the next situation that arises. Like each generation before them, the children of the 1970s can only respond to the world as they find it. Not surprisingly, their experience of impermanence and unpredictability has taught them one big, central lesson: *keep your options open.* Whether they are thinking about a course of study, a job, a sexual partner, a political party, a set of religious beliefs, or even whether they'll be home for dinner tonight, they have decided to remain as non-committal as possible, for as long as possible. Because they are the children of change, they do not fear the future or the further changes it may bring; but they know that change *will* come, so stability and predictability – even as goals – seem rather incongruous.

Yet, however well they might be adapting to the idea of constant change, they cannot escape its destabilising impact: you have to be strong to stay flexible and not all members of this generation have managed to summon the strength required. In the meantime, one of the most effective coping mechanisms they have discovered is to adopt the stance of 'interested bystanders', awaiting the moment when it feels right to them to exercise one option or another and to take centre stage in their own drama.

The Options Generation are often criticised for apathy, or for premature conservatism. Their tendency to hang back from conventional commitments can easily be mistaken for a dismissive attitude of disengagement when, in fact, it is simply a sign of their assumption that the world is unlikely to go on as it is. There is no discernible lack of passion or energy, but their enthusiasms are expressed in less predictable ways than was the case for their parents or grandparents. The Options Generation like making it up as they go along.

When their grandparents were at this stage in the life cycle, they were moving steadily – perhaps inexorably – towards what seemed like a preordained sequence of events: marriage and a family (or, for 20 per cent of them, remaining single, perhaps to look after ailing parents); a long-term career for men and single women, and, for those who *did* marry, a lifetime spent as a male breadwinner or a female housekeeper and nurturer of children.

For the Boomer parents of the Options Generation, this stage of the life cycle was marked by a voracious impatience to have everything, and to have it *now*. (They thought material prosperity was their birthright, but that there might not be much future in which to enjoy it.)

The rising generation, by contrast, are ineffably patient. They know there will be a future and, although their predictions – economic and environmental – about their country and the planet tend to be pessimistic, they assume that 'it will be okay for *me*'. There is plenty of time. There is no reason to rush, because the kaleidoscope keeps moving and the patterns are not set for long. But, when the time comes for commitment (no matter how narrowly focused or short-term it may be), they are confident that they will be able to pick the moment.

THE 'INDEPENDENCE' PARADOX

So how does it feel to be a member of this generation so intent on keeping its options open?

The first of the many ironies and contradictions which characterise the Options Generation is that they are the most dependent generation of young Australians in our history and yet they rate 'independence' as one of their top priorities, and they report *feeling* highly independent.

They have stayed at school for longer than any generation in our history; stayed at home for longer than their parents' generation did;

moved on to the dole in larger numbers, and sooner, than any other generation of Australians. It is a generation accustomed to being 'looked after' by educational institutions, by parents, and by welfare, well into their twenties.

Yet their obsession with options means they are determined to live life on their own terms. They expect to build *flexibility* into their plans and that, in turn, raises a central dilemma: if they stay at home, they have to be 'under the thumb' to some extent because their parents resist the idea of home being treated like a low-rent (or free) boarding house. On the other hand, the personal freedom which is thought to be fundamental to true independence – and which can't be achieved while still living at home – costs money, and money is the big issue for many members of this generation.

If they are still at school or involved in post-secondary studies, they are likely to be heavily dependent on their parents for funds (even if they might have some other source of income – via Austudy, for example). If they are unemployed, then living away from home is only an option if they can gather a like-minded group around them and pool their welfare payments to fund the rent and other living expenses.

Even if they are in full-time or part-time employment, many members of the Options Generation quite like the idea of lingering at home for a while, simply to enable them to build up their funds so that they can exercise some of the options available to them, such as travel, a period spent 'drifting', or even paying a deposit on a house or flat.

So the strong emotional urge to symbolise independence by moving away from the parental home is often outweighed by the financial pressure to stay put. According to the Australian Bureau of Statistics, about 80 per cent of single people between the ages of 15 and 24 still live at home with one or both parents. In the past ten years, the number of 20- to 24-year-olds living at home has jumped from 29 to 38 per cent. An implication of these figures is that one traditional 'rite of passage' – moving out – is being postponed by many young adults to the point where the distinction between adolescence and adulthood blurs, and the 'moment' of independence is replaced by a process of gradual negotiation.

Whether young adults feel sufficiently independent while still living at home is largely a function of the quality of their relationship with their parents, and the ability of both parties to negotiate a reasonable arrangement. In some cases, young adults report that their parents set them free to come and go as they wish, without restraint and without asking any questions. In other cases, they have found that it is necessary to lead two lives: 'You behave one way at home, and another when you're out . . . your parents would die if they knew what you were up to.'

Many people on both sides of this relationship report tension. As the young adults develop completely independent social lives – including sexual relationships – the working-out of mutually acceptable 'house rules' is a challenge which not everyone can meet:

> My relationship with my mother has changed. When I was living at home, things got a bit tense because I was doing stuff . . . but since I've moved out, we've got along really well. It's not that we fought, but the air was getting thicker.

> Let's face it, we're living a charmed life. Our parents are basically keeping us, and we can do pretty much what we like. You are mainly treated like an adult, but you are supported as if you are still a kid. But you do have to limit your freedom a bit if you are going to stay with your parents into your twenties. You have to play it by their rules to a certain extent, although, personally, I feel there's a point at which my room is clean enough, and I just want to go out and have a good time.

The trickiest negotiating point is, however, not over the cleanliness of a bedroom or the hour of returning home, or the giving of adequate notice for being present or absent from meals. The real sticking-point is sex: in particular, the question of whether sexual partners should be allowed to sleep overnight in the parental home. Buried among the diverse solutions to this problem is a recurring theme which is perhaps surprising: parents (fathers, in particular) seem more relaxed about their sons having a sexual partner to stay overnight than they are about their daughters doing the same thing. Clearly, vestiges of the old double standard can still be found:

My father would flip if I had my boyfriend home to spend the night. But I can go to his place, and no one seems to turn a hair. I suppose, from my father's point of view, it's a case of 'out of sight . . .'

My parents were really terrific about having my girlfriend stay the night. They knew her really well, and we have been going together for a couple of years, so it was no particular big deal. They are much more concerned about drugs than sex.

Discussion of sexuality and contraception and things like that is so much more open now – even at home – but there are still plenty of couples who realise that their parents would expect them to get married if they wanted to sleep together. One of my girlfriends is already married and she's only 20, and it was just because she and her boyfriend weren't prepared to defy her parents.

My son brings all his girlfriends home to stay. Last night I was doing the dishes about 11.00 p.m. and I heard the key in the door and I thought, 'That's funny'. It turned out that he had given the key to a new girlfriend. How many others has he given the key to? It's not secure.

When my son asked could his girlfriend live with us, I said, 'That's fine, but there have to be some rules. I don't want any kinky sex or to hear any strange noises.' And he said, 'Mum, we probably won't even do it here.'

The issue of moving out or staying at home is inextricably linked to the problem of employment. In some parts of Australia, unemployment for the Options Generation exceeds 50 per cent and, with only 20 per cent of school leavers going to university, there is a large pool of young people for whom the goal of independence lies beyond the giant hurdle of unemployment:

Unemployment isn't too bad. There are stages. The first couple of months is good pay, on the dole, and having a good time. You don't have to get up and do anything . . . but after a while, everything gets boring – even partying gets boring. And you get a bit lazier and your motivation goes right down. I know for myself, if I'm doing something, I'll get up early and do it, but if I'm not, I'll just lay around and be lazy most of the day.

You don't really have as much leisure when you're on the dole – you sit around more, but most of the things you want to do cost money.

After I left school, I sat on the dole for a couple of months, got bored of that, and got a job. I just couldn't stand sitting around doing nothing all day. A job gives you more money to spend on weekends. I'm happier now I am working.

It's not very complicated: a job brings money and money brings the yearned-for sense of independence. Whether the young person is living at home or not, money in the pocket is the real issue:

Work is a lot better than bludging on the dole, but I don't really care what I do. I was going to do carpentry, but I got this job at a truss factory and it was totally boring. So now I am going to have a go at crane-driving. You don't want to work, but after a while of sitting at home and getting the dole, you realise that work is not all that bad. It keeps your time occupied and it gives you some sense of achievement. If you're good at a job and stick with it, it makes you feel good. And you get paid for it, too.

This is a generation growing up with the idea of job insecurity firmly fixed in their minds. They know that it is probably unrealistic to set too much store by a particular line of work. Even when they have a job, they are as ready as they can be for the possibility of losing it and having to move on to something else.

Independence, therefore, is a larger concept than it was for their parents or grandparents. Independence means being able to handle flexibility, voluntarily and involuntarily. Independence means having a sense of yourself which is not tied to a job. Independence means achieving a state of mind where, devoid of the frameworks that gave security to your grandparents (and guidance, at least, to your parents), you can still 'hang loose' and wait, or, when the time comes, 'go for it'.

MORAL BOUNDARY RIDERS

Rebellious and antisocial behaviour among adolescents is always a sign that their personal war of independence has not yet been won. For the Boomers, full-blown teenage rebelliousness was relatively short-lived because a buoyant labour market and a rapid rate of economic growth paved the way to early financial independence. The Boomers couldn't wait to leave home, to travel or just to 'flat'.

For the Options Generation, by contrast, the medium-term prospects for financial independence are more bleak, and so the classic teenage badges of quasi-independence – sex, alcohol and drug abuse, non-conformist hair, clothes and language – are worn with elan and zeal, often into the mid-twenties.

Further complicating the situation is the fact that this is probably the first generation of young Australians to grow up without having had a moral framework clearly espoused and unambiguously articulated by their parents. The Boomers are themselves still searching for a more satisfying code than the feel-good ethic of the 1960s, so it is not surprising that their offspring have been left to develop their own moral codes and to establish their own sets of values. In the process, a good deal of moral 'boundary riding' goes on – testing the limits – as they accumulate the kind of experience they will subsequently use as a foundation for whatever moral framework they ultimately construct.

In the meantime, those at the younger end of the Options

Generation are as pleased as any teenagers ever were to find that they are capable of shocking their parents, impressing their peers and even surprising themselves by their own audacity:

At 18, you are out to enjoy yourself and have a ball, which means getting very drunk, meeting new people – especially guys – and having stories to tell your friends about the night before . . . all the dramas about who's kissing who and who did I see out doing this.

We all go out in a big group and you sort of love everyone, but not in a sexual way. But after a few drinks, you sometimes forget what sort of love you feel for a guy, and have sex with him.

Eighteen or 19 is supposed to be your sexual prime, so it's when you want it most. You're on the prowl, like a cat – you've got your sensors going, left, right and centre.

I should be able to save, but last year I just went mad and blew all my money on the thrills of the time . . . smoking pot and taking girls out. I've thought about saving, but I just can't do it. I have to keep going out every night.

Part of the thrill of boundary riding is taking the well-known risks involved. For today's teens, that thrill acquires a harder edge as they recognise that a growing number of risks – especially those associated with drug abuse and unprotected sex – are potentially lethal:

I'm scared shitless about AIDS. I'm scared enough not to have the test, because it might tell me what I don't want to know.

The driving techniques of people in our age group are a worry. You think you're young, you're energetic . . . so it's all right to speed, and you don't learn unless you go through a personal experience. The girls are conscious of not driving after they've had too much to drink, but a lot of the boys aren't. They have

147

got away with doing it so many times that they just keep going. I hope something happens to one of them, so they get a shock and wake up.

The drug scene can be really scary, like that girl who died from Ecstasy. That one was an accident, but some people get serious – get totally hooked – and they can basically wipe themselves out before they're 20.

The sense of living dangerously at a time of social dislocation and high unemployment, without a strong moral code in place, is heady stuff. And yet, as they move into their early and mid-twenties, the Options Generation do begin the process of clarifying their values and even of narrowing the range of options they want to exercise. Even if they are still hanging back from the sort of commitment their parents were so keen to make at the same age, they are beginning to sense that life is taking shape, after all, and that patterns of behaviour are being established. In other words, a framework of values is being constructed, however casually or unconsciously.

In *Reality Isn't What It Used To Be,* Walter Truett Anderson supports the view that human beings are essentially social animals who develop systems of morality as naturally as they eat and breathe. Anderson is therefore quite sanguine about the moral prospects of the generation growing up in a postmodern world of subjectivity and relativity:

For those who think of moral development in this way, a social environment of conflicting realities and conflicting moralities is, at least potentially, an excellent matrix in which to grow people of highly-developed moral character. Conflict – certain kinds of conflict, conflict in which moral issues are made explicit – can create the situation in which people become capable of moving from one stage [of moral development] to the next. Morality, then, is the product of hard-won wisdom, a way of being that expresses wherever a person happens to be along the (hopefully) never-ending path of understanding and reunderstanding life, constructing and reconstructing the rules of relationship between self and others.[1]

The weakness in Anderson's argument – at least for the Options Generation – is that in many of the circumstances in which today's young Australians are testing themselves, moral issues are *not* made explicit. Nevertheless, to hear some older members of the Options Generation tell it, the experience of prolonged experimentation in the late teens and early twenties does, indeed, produce a certain moral tension, and a recognition that they have come to a series of forks in the road.

For those who tumbled out of the education system without any real sense of achievement or purpose, or whose family circumstances are so unsupportive as to be discouraging, or who feel themselves to be irrevocably rebuffed by a hostile labour market, the pathway leading to despair is attractive, and perhaps even irresistible. Many members of the Options Generation have sunk into feelings of depression and alienation bordering on suicide – sometimes actually crossing that line:

I think we're the bored generation. Everyone I know is bored. Being exposed to everything and wanting so much . . . you get kind of bored. People are just getting bored of the same old thing – go to the pub, get drunk, play darts – or go to the disco, take speed and dance all night to a computer beat. To me, it has no substance at all.

But others, sniffing an opportunity, decide to cash in their experience and move on:

When I was 18 or 19, I'd be out till three or four in the morning, then have a shower and go straight to work. I was wrecked. I don't do that any more. For a start, at 23, you're smarter with your money.

I shudder when I think of some of the things I did a few

years ago. I am lucky to have survived, I guess. Your priorities certainly change once you get into your twenties. You think a bit more about the future, and not just about the moment. Back then, I didn't really care what I did. Now, I'm conscious of the fact that I've got to make something of my life.

Frankly, I got sick of being sick . . .

This is not to suggest that Options people miraculously turn conservative on their 23rd birthday; far from it. For many of them, though, there does seem to be a rather rapid transit from hedonism bordering on nihilism to something more positive and constructive. Perhaps, as Anderson suggests, the experience of living in some social and moral chaos may actually accelerate the spontaneous evolution of a set of functional values:

I don't suppose I believe in anything, really, except myself. I want to make something of myself. I can't believe how unfocused I've been up till now . . . just going with the flow. It was great while it lasted, but eventually you've got to pull yourself out of it and decide to do something. It doesn't really matter what it is, and I probably won't do any of the things my parents were hoping I'd do. But I'll do something.

Some respond to the turbulence of life in this age of discontinuity quite differently: the Options Generation have played their part in the rise of religious fundamentalism as some teenagers and young adults, feeling uncomfortable with too much flexibility and too little certainty, seek a ready-made framework supplied by one of the mainstream religions. Those who discover fundamentalist religion in their early or mid-teens might shock their parents with a different kind of boundary riding, by going to the limits of religious fervour.

Since fundamentalism of any kind – religious, economic, environmental, political – generates its own focus and its own certainties, this is a particularly appealing option for those young people who find the prospect of 'hanging loose' altogether too demanding.

In the end, fundamentalism is an expression of impatience to reach a conclusion rather than tarry on the journey and explore some of the ambiguities along the way. Not surprisingly, the very pressures which have spawned the 'options' mentality in so many young adults have stimulated a contradictory response in others.

But whether the response is nihilism, fundamentalism or a desire to 'live to the max', the unifying theme here is that the Options Generation are determined to dictate their own terms. The Boomers were attracted to the same idea, but were swept along by their material prosperity; the Options Generation have no real alternative but to work it out, gradually, for themselves. Sooner or later, though, most of the moral boundary-riders come back from the edge.

MARRIAGE AND FAMILY? NOT YET, THANKS

A 'happy marriage' continues to be a virtually universal ideal, even though it is constantly being reinterpreted. Whereas the Lucky Generation saw marriage, to some extent, as an end in itself (or, at least, as an unvaryingly stable institution), the Boomers developed a less rigid view of marriage: they placed more emphasis on the quality of the relationship and correspondingly less emphasis on the integrity of the institution itself. The Options Generation have carried their Boomer parents' thinking one stage further: they are even more committed to the idea that the quality of a personal relationship is the paramount thing, and marriage is a secondary question. For the Options Generation, 'happy marriage' might well mean 'ten years of happiness', it might mean a short or long period of cohabitation – with or without the tying of a legal knot – or it might mean a lifelong commitment to one partner.

The ideal marriage, for the rising generation, is sometimes described as 'being married to my best friend' and it is clear that members of the Options Generation do tend to develop enduring friendships with young people of both sexes – more than was characteristic of either their parents' or grandparents' generations at the same stage in the life cycle.

Boomers were keen to pair off at an early age; the Options Generation are more likely to 'stick with the group' and to maintain strong social connections with young men and young women – sometimes including sexual partners, but often involving close and even intimate personal relationships that are non-sexual. (The sexually impatient Boomers often have trouble accepting that their offspring's mixed-sex living arrangements in university colleges or flats, or on casual 'weekends away', do not necessarily incorporate sexual activity.)

Nevertheless, the difficulties of making generalisations about the Options Generation are very apparent when we listen to their views on marriage. Some of them are determined to have a full-scale white wedding: perhaps, as Boomer parents determinedly cling to the symbols of their own youth, some members of the Options Generation are feeling the need to draw on more traditional symbols and rituals to mark their progress towards adulthood. Others seem relaxed about the blurring of the distinctions between adolescence and adulthood: when it comes to marriage, they are prepared to let experimental cohabitation gradually evolve into a more permanent arrangement, never needing to mark the precise moment of transition.

Between those two extremes, every imaginable view of marriage can be found. The two recurring themes, though, are that the Options Generation are attracted to the idea of postponing marriage – keeping your options open – and they are determined that, if and when the time comes, they will 'do' marriage in their own way:

I'd like to be married by the age of 30 and have two kids by the age of 35. I don't want to be an older mother. You never know what's around the corner, but there's no point in getting married until you are at least 25.

I broke up with my girlfriend three months ago because things were too good . . . the next step would have been marriage. We knew we were too young. I want to be married before I'm 35, but not before 25.

Living together is not frowned upon as it used to be. I think you should live together before marriage, to see if you're compatible. I've been accused of being non-committal, but I don't think that living together has to lead to marriage. It's just an extension of going out together.

For late teenagers, the idea of being an 'older parent' is appalling, so there is some interest in finding the best moment to marry and have children: they want to be old enough to be sure they are ready to 'settle down', but they don't want to be so old that they will feel remote from their children:

I don't want to be too old when I have my kids. I don't want to be playing cricket with my walking-stick at 60 years of age. On the other hand, I don't want to rush in. So many marriages fail that I want to be sure before I take that step. So, I suppose I will get married and have kids in my thirties, but I'd like to test the waters before then.

The Options Generation talk about the desirability of marriage, but they stop short of thinking of it as inevitable. Current predictions by the Australian Institute of Family Studies suggest that by the year 2000, the proportion of women not married by the time they reach 35 years of age will exceed 20 per cent, a level higher than at any other time in Australian history.

In any case, in spite of the desire of some young people to maximise the symbolism of a wedding, the *real* milestone is parenthood:

Whether you get married or not is not the big deal it used to be. People divorce fairly easily . . . or they just split up, if they have only been living together. But having children changes everything. So you would want to be sure that you were in a pretty stable relationship – and you had some financial security behind you – before you think about having children. I'd like to be committed to my work for a number of years so I can get the most out of it, but once I have less of a desire to prove things,

I can think about other things and be able to spend more time with a family. I wouldn't want to have a family until I could do that.

The Options Generation look at their parents' marriages and frequently decide that, when it's their turn, they will try to handle things rather differently. They are inclined to see their parents as having been in too much of a hurry, as having accepted 'the strain' of children too early in their married lives and, as a result, as having closed off too many options too soon. The Boomers themselves believe they exercised far more freedom of choice than their own parents had been able to do, but their children see them as having been highly conformist in their approach to marriage and parenthood, even though the fabric of family life has been shredded in a growing number of cases. Indeed, the rising generation are inclined to think that 'too much, too soon' is actually a prescription for failure in marriage and family life: they prefer to approach it steadily, cautiously and tentatively. When the time comes, they want to feel that they have both the emotional and the financial security to be able to make a go of it.

All of this might seem to contradict their more relaxed and accepting attitude towards divorce. (The predictions are that for their generation, the divorce rate might reach 45 per cent.) For the members of the Options Generation, though, there is no contradiction: they expect to be committed to a partner when the time comes to have children, but they acknowledge – with less dreamy sentimentality than they might discern in their parents – that some marriages are not 'forever'; that ten years might be 'a good innings'; that children's needs should be taken into account but not allowed to 'destroy your life'.

If this sounds a little more callous and cynical than the attitudes of Boomers towards the task of parenting, then that seems consistent with an emerging attitude in the Options Generation: they are inclined to see their parents as having worked hard – even 'too hard' – to support and educate a family; they like to imagine that when the time comes, they will want more out of life than 'slaving for the kids'.

In this, they are echoing an attitude already strongly established among post-Boomers – that generation born in the 1960s, who are tucked comfortably and inconspicuously between the Boomers and their children. Post-Boomers are quietly determined to enjoy the fruits of their parents' labour to provide for them: they appreciate their parents' devotion and support without wanting to follow their example of a life which seems to have been overly child-centred. Similarly, they are prepared to 'cash in' on the pioneering efforts of the Boomers, without wanting to be caught up in too much heavy social pioneering of their own. Post-Boomers are taking a generational breather: they want to make an art form out of 'creating a lifestyle', and they have declared a generational change of direction: 'Our parents worked for us, but we're working for ourselves'.

Time will tell. Parenthood is, of course, one of life's great mind-changing experiences. Nevertheless, many members of the Options Generation neither envy their parents nor hope to emulate them. They criticise them for having closed off too many options and for having created lives which seem to their children to be unnecessarily complex and burdensome. While the children are grateful to their parents for the sacrifices they have made and the support they have given, they are often unimpressed by their parents' example:

Mum and Dad are just getting on top of things financially now. I'd like to be in that position younger. I can see myself as financially secure in my mid-thirties. They got started much more quickly . . . they were out of school and into a job, then married and getting on with raising a family. We are taking a much more relaxed approach to all that, aren't we? I don't expect to be 'getting started' the way they were until I'm close to 30. As a matter of fact, I don't think I will ever achieve the same level of prosperity as my mum and dad, and it doesn't really worry me. I'm not inclined to get on that treadmill. They are a lot better off than my grandparents were . . . and I would be quite happy to do as well as my grandparents did. They seem more relaxed than my parents, anyway.

Our parents' generation were really incredibly prosperous, when you come to think of it. Would it be such a big deal if we didn't do as well as that? It's not bothering me. I like having more choices, more options . . . the ability to change from one thing to another is more important to me than settling into the grind of a mortgage and one career in one job. I admire my parents for what they did, but I don't want to end up the way they have. Frankly, I think it would be a bit boring. I wouldn't mind the comfort, but I'd want more out of life than that.

It remains to be seen whether the Options Generation will be able to manage their lives in the way they presently intend. Many of them know that their employment prospects are so bleak that financial leanness is likely to be a permanent feature of their lives; others are so optimistic about their personal prospects that they assume they will be able to acquire financial security, even if it eludes other members of their generation. The range of expectations about material prosperity is as wide as the range of this generation's expectations about everything else.

The significant thread running through talk of their future is that the Options Generation will have more *flexibility* and more *freedom* in their lives than they believe their parents have experienced – and certainly more than was available to their grandparents. Some of their expectations are rosy and optimistic, some are dark and despairing, but there is a strong impression that this is a generation determined to do it their way; to shape whatever opportunities are available to their own needs and aspirations.

When it comes to marriage and family, therefore, the Options Generation are as determined to hang loose as they are about study, careers, or the direction of life itself.

Accordingly, the expectation that they will marry is accompanied by an almost equally universal expectation that they will have several serious sexual relationships along the way to marriage, or even *after* their first marriage. Some older members of the Options Generation say things like 'I'm on my first marriage', with the clear expectation that even if the marriage seems happy and stable, nothing can be taken for granted:

> I met my boyfriend last year and that made it a really amazing year. He is one of the most important things in my life. I love him, and we are great friends. But we have great respect for each other's independence and thoughts ... I hate the idea of my mother's generation, that women would get married and that is what would make them secure. I want to be secure on my own, before I think about marrying someone. You have to be whole in yourself before you can have a successful marriage. This thing of having emptiness inside and having to fill that gap is not my idea of marriage.

Of course, romantic love plays its ever-present role:

> I've had the same girlfriend for three months. It's a weird experience for me to be in ... all attempts I've had to date have ended in disaster. We met by chance, and it's gone on from there, much to my surprise. But it's made me a happier person, so something must be right. She is very important in my life – more important than I like to admit, perhaps. She kind of balances a lot of things out and she has given me a new and better way of looking at life. With her, I can cope better with other aspects of my life, by getting that relaxing side of things.

For the Options Generation, love and marriage certainly do *not* go together like the proverbial horse and carriage: love is wonderful and marriage is a pleasing (if generally distant) prospect, but one does not lead inexorably to the other. Among young adult women, in particular, there is strong resistance to the idea of inevitable marriage – especially if it is being used as a passport to identity or security; they will marry, they say, because they want to enter into the married state with the partner of their choice, not because society or their parents or their peers are urging them to get married.

There are exceptions, of course: some members of the Options Generation are unashamedly desperate to use marriage as an escape from present unhappiness, boredom or loneliness. The difference between such attitudes today and the same attitudes in earlier generations is that they would currently be regarded by their peers as aberrant and even 'disgusting'.

Young adults believe that when it comes to the idea of marriage, their priorities are quite different from their parents'. They see no urgency about marriage, and although they regard it as a conventional state, they are open to a wide range of unconventional ways of approaching it and managing it.

As they see it, their parents typically married and 'settled', *then* began working to establish themselves financially and to develop their relationship. For the Options Generation, the ideal is to do it all the other way around: they like to think of themselves as becoming established financially, developing a strong and successful emotional relationship, and finally – on those twin foundations – making the decision about whether or not to get married. That decision, when it comes, is as likely to be a decision about having children as about making a lifelong commitment to a partner.

Members of the Options Generation recognise the shakiness of marriage as an institution. For some, that leads to the proposition that 'we might as well give it a go'; for others, that 'we might as well *not* rush into it'. In both cases, there is an edge of realism which the Boomers might judge to be lacking in 'romance':

Our parents had children at a younger age which has its advantages, I suppose. They are out and about now, still keeping up with the latest trends, whereas we will still be raising children when we are their age. But there are advantages in having babies after 30. You've got your house and your car and, when you do have babies, you can really enjoy them.

I will bring my children up very differently from the way my parents did it. They were too involved, too conscientious. I would like to give my kids a bit more freedom, and I would like to be a bit more relaxed about being a parent than my mum was. Also, there's no way I want to be caught having a job at the time when I am trying to look after young children. It's better to handle these things separately – work for a while, take time off for kids, and then go back to work. My mother is exhausted every day, and I am determined that I won't live like that.

We are having kids a lot later than our parents were, and I think this has a lot to do with why we are staying selfish for a longer period. But I don't think we should put the previous generation up on a pedestal – they just did what they had to do.

Let's face it, people have got a bigger wish-list now, before they get married. In ten years' time, I would like the house well and truly paid off, and at least a couple of kids. I'd like the house paid off first, not like my parents who struggled to do that. You are more free to work things out your own way, these days. You can please yourself, you can make it up as you go along. I'll bet you we all get married, but I'll also bet that things will turn out very differently for all of us . . .

For the Boomers – a generation who prided themselves on placing such a high value on 'love' and took the business of relationships so seriously – it must be particularly galling to hear their children talking about their determination to have 'better marriages' and, indeed, 'better relationships' than their parents had. Members of the Options Generation often remark on what they perceive as the joylessness in their parents' lives, often attributed to excessive busyness, but sometimes also interpreted as the price their parents paid for having rushed into marriage on the crest of a wave of sexual impatience – or even impatience for the experience of parenthood – without having established a solid basis of emotional compatibility and sheer human friendship beforehand.

Even more galling, perhaps, would be the rising generation's assertion that they are determined to have more relaxed relationships with their children than they have experienced with their own parents:

I certainly want to have a better marriage than my parents have. They seem quite comfortable with each other but that's about it. I would expect to be much closer than that to a person, if I was going to settle down and marry them – even if it wasn't going to last a lifetime. If you were only marrying for sex, what hope would you have?

I always found my parents a bit distant from my brother and me. I would want my children to be able to approach me in time of trouble, but there is no way I would be able to talk to my own parents. My father is still studying, for a start, and my mother races around like a scalded cat when she comes home from work. You don't get the feeling that you would be particularly welcome if you had something serious you wanted to discuss.

My personal relationships – with my husband if I ever have one, and with my kids – would be much more important to me than what kind of car I drove or whether I owned my house. In fact, I think my standard of living might be lower than my parents' but I wouldn't mind that if I was leading a satisfying life.

In lots of ways, I imagine I will have a very different life from my parents. What they've got is great. They are still together and they are still in love, and they are materially well off. But I can't see myself finding someone and staying with him for the rest of my life. My parents are from the generation that you're meant to be together for as long as you live.

My parents would be very hurt if they heard me say this, but I think they have overdone it a bit on the parenting thing. It's great to have them around, and everything, but it's not all that relaxed. I would like to be more relaxed with my own kids, if I have any. I don't think I'll be wanting to hang around them so much, and ask so many questions. One of my friends said that parents should be seen and not heard . . . I think she's got a point. Everything is too important to my mum and dad. I'm

glad they are interested and everything, but I wish they would
trust me a bit more to make up my own mind about things.

As the older members of the Options Generation anticipate parenthood, they certainly sound as if they intend to take a rather more
relaxed approach to child care than the Boomers did. They are
more relaxed about making use of child-care facilities than their
own mothers were, and it is now being estimated that as many as
one-third of the children of the Options Generation will spend vast
tracts of time in child-care facilities before starting school. Writing
in the *Good Weekend*, Sally Loane calculated that 'a child can
spend up to 12 500 hours in child care before starting school, only
500 hours less than he or she will spend in lessons in an entire 13
years of schooling'.[2]

The effect of that on the children can't yet be assessed, though
Sally Loane quoted a Melbourne teacher as saying:

> You can always pick a child who has been to child care. They
> have well-developed survival skills; they know how to get atten-
> tion. They are often uncooperative, aggressive and secretive,
> and jaded and cynical about learning.

In an Australian Institute of Family Studies report, *Today's Child
Care, Tomorrow's Children*, Gay Ochiltree and Don Edgar
commented:

> Children who have had extensive experience of group care are
> accustomed to competing with others to get their own way.
> They are likely to have become less conforming or good and
> tend to be more demanding of their teacher's attention than
> children who have spent most of their preschool years at home
> with their mothers. They are more independent, more likely to
> question authority and more gregarious.[3]

Quentin Bryce, head of the National Childcare Accreditation Council, puts it more positively: 'I'm always struck by the sociability of

the children. They come up, sit on your lap, pat your hair, tell you stories.'[4]

Only about 40 per cent of Australia's children under four years of age are cared for in the family home by a parent. Apart from those in formal child-care, the rest are looked after by a relative or babysitter.

But whether Options Generation parents decide that one of them will stay at home to care for the children, or that both of them will continue working, they are determined to make their own decisions in ways that reflect the particular features of their own circumstances. To this generation, 'normal' is 'whatever feels right for me'.

The main thing that the Options Generation aspire to, as parents, is that as their own children reach adolescence, there will be more openness between the generations, and a greater willingness on both sides to broach any subject, however difficult. This, of course, was the same dream that Boomer parents had: the difference is that they thought the way to facilitate communication with their children was to 'stay close', whereas the Options Generation speak as if they will want to be 'available' rather than being so intently 'involved'.

This points to another important difference between the Options Generation and their Boomer parents. Whereas Boomer women, in particular, spoke about the multiplicity of choices and roles available to them and seemed eager to embrace many of those roles simultaneously, Options women have set themselves a different goal: they, too, want to experience the full range of roles available to them, but not necessarily all at once. At this early stage, they sound as if they will be prepared to be one thing, *then* another, *then* something else, rather than everything at once. This attitude is shaping their approach to marriage, to parenthood and to work: everything is possible; everything is an option; nothing needs to be settled quickly, comprehensively or irrevocably. Hang loose! Stay cool!

IS THE GENDER REVOLUTION OVER? NOT QUITE

One of the convictions the Options Generation carry easily with them into adulthood is that men and women are equal but different; that equal opportunities for men and women should be taken for granted; that men and women should be able to negotiate roles and responsibilities – at home and at work – in ways which respect the needs and preferences of each.

Boomer women who went to the barricades for feminism might wish that their offspring were more grimly determined about all this, and more grateful to them for having fomented such a successful gender revolution. In fact, the women of the Options Generation acknowledge that there has been a dramatic change between their parents' generation and their own: for a start, they are no longer subject to the 'production-line' process which would once have moved women automatically into early marriage and the rearing of children, and out of the workforce. Yet, in spite of the fact that most of their mothers have combined motherhood with at least some paid employment outside the home, they are still inclined to think of their parents' generation as having been victims of that production line – at least in the early years of their adulthood – even if not to the same extent as their grandparents' generation.

Early Boomer women may have thought of themselves as being better educated than their own mothers and as having had more life-choices available to them, but they concede that those choices didn't really open up for them until they left school. By contrast, Options women speak of a wide range of choices having been available to them from their mid-teens. For a start, they have always known that they were as likely as any boy to complete their secondary education; the thought that boys might have received preferential treatment in the extent or content of their secondary and tertiary education would seem grossly unfair – even laughable – to them.

Facing adulthood, Options women regard themselves as being under no pressure to conform to any particular stereotype, whether traditional or contemporary, and they strongly resist any notion that in order to be true to the feminist cause they have to carry certain banners, mouth certain slogans, or plan their lives in a certain way. When they face the prospect of motherhood, for example, they are perfectly relaxed about the possibility of being full-time mothers *or* combining motherhood with paid employment (either full-time or part-time), *or* sharing with their partners in part-time parenting and part-time breadwinning. There is no agreed norm to which Options women feel they must conform.

Education is regarded as the key to all this, but so is a kind of 'social awareness' in which members of the Options Generation take great pride. Whereas the young women of the Options Generation might not regard their mothers as having been pioneering feminists, there is widespread appreciation of the fact that their mothers have encouraged them to embrace the choices available to them: sometimes they accept this encouragement uncritically, but sometimes they regard it as a sign of their own mothers' frustrations at the limited choices which were available to them at the same age:

> *My mother brought me up to have a lot of self-respect – she made me feel as though I could do anything I want to do. I realise that women have the choice now, whether to be a housewife or go out and work. And men are even starting to acknowledge that housework is a real job.*
>
> *I think my father still has some rather old-fashioned attitudes towards women, but he has gone along with my mother's belief that I should have all the same opportunities as my brother. And I have, too. At least males aren't looking at us and thinking we should be in the kitchen, like they were when my parents got married.*

It would be convenient to be able to report that males in the Options Generation have reached precisely the same point as females in their thinking about gender roles and responsibilities, but it's not quite that simple. It is true that young men appear to understand gender issues more readily and comprehensively than their fathers or grandfathers did, and they appear to be sincere in their assertion that men and women should have equal opportunities and should take equal responsibility for parenting. But the problem for the men of the Options Generation is that they have been presented with messages from their mothers which have often been in conflict with the *example* of their fathers. They have accepted their mothers' propositions about sexual equality but they have observed their fathers acting in ways which don't always match that rhetoric.

Inevitably, therefore, there are lingering confusions among the young men of this generation as they try to come to terms with the expectations of their female friends, without 'slipping back' into prejudices they have acquired from older males:

> *Two years ago, I went out with a girl for three months and she was very nice and then she asked me, 'What are your intentions with me?' After three months! Girls are sometimes funny. They talk to each other: 'Do this to him . . . push him into this corner.' It's like insider trading. I'm all for equality between the sexes, but men and women often have very different attitudes when it comes to sex and relationships.*

> *Women can go off and have their careers and they are getting good jobs, but where does that leave opportunities for us guys, when we are 30 and wanting to have children? To a certain extent, women's lib has gone too far. It's becoming unbalanced. For us, the opportunity for promotion is now getting harder than it was 20 years ago. While we're messing around and having fun, women are getting on with it . . . and they're the ones getting the promotions.*

Nevertheless, women of the Options Generation seem generally relaxed about the attitudes and values of their male friends, and they feel more closely in touch with young male attitudes than their mothers recall having been at the same stage. It is a matter of great pride among both male and female members of the Options Generation

that 'guys and girls can be good friends' and that close personal relationships can cross the gender barrier without necessarily implying
sexual attraction or entanglements.

This is presumably one of the positive outcomes of the women's
movement. Young women appear to be more interested in fostering
'platonic' relationships with boys than their mothers were. They
are comfortable about joining peer groups which comprise both
males and females. They enjoy an active social life which includes
quite intimate relationships with a number of boys, none of which
might be sexual in character.

Of course, plenty of adolescents and young adults do have a
series of exclusive sexual relationships as well. But their discussion
of their socio-sexual lives suggests that mixed-gender, non-sexual
social groupings (and even pairings) are non-threatening and more
relaxed than the Boomer women recall from their own adolescence.
The young women of the Options Generation, in particular, relish
the sense of confidence and personal power which they obtain from
being able to develop relationships with young men, in a group setting, where no expectation of sexual favours is created.

Indeed, it has become characteristic of young Options women to
speak with warm appreciation of the boys and young men who have
become like 'extra brothers' to them, and to refer to the pleasure
they take in socialising with boys who have become real friends
without being tagged 'boyfriends':

> In our group on the weekend, we've got guys and girls, but we
> are more like brothers and sisters. We are all very close, but we
> are just friends. We don't expect sex or anything from each
> other. We just have a lot of fun and talk to each other and be
> with one another. We talk about sex a lot, and we are really
> open . . . some of the people do pair off. But it is really great
> having a boy for a close friend. You get a different point of view
> talking to him than you do talking to your girlfriends.

Some young women in the Options Generation even profess to
believe that non-sexual relationships with boys can be more relaxed

and more honest than their relationships with other girls, being less emotionally intense, less competitive, and less subject to the pressure of same-sex peers.

This sense of feeling 'powerful and relaxed' with young males gives the women of the Options Generation another advantage: they believe that when they are subjected to sexual pressure, they are able to make more confident choices about whether or not to engage in sexual intercourse. To hear them tell it, Options women believe that they only engage in sexual activity if they really want to – whether they happen to be 'in love' or not – whereas they believe that in their mothers' generation, girls were too easily pressured into sexual activity which was against their inclination or, at least, against their better judgement.

Neither the males nor the females of the Options Generation appear to attach quite the same moral significance to sexual activity as their parents and, most particularly, their grandparents did. To people now in their late teens and early twenties, sexual activity is rarely likely to be regarded as 'wrong' even if it is engaged in with someone who is not regarded as a potential long-term partner. Being 'in love' is still a widely accepted, though by no means universal, prerequisite for sexual intercourse, but sex is a far less mysterious subject than it used to be and the decision to engage in sexual activity appears to be less significant than it was even for the sexually-permissive Boomers.

Here again, though, there is the widest imaginable diversity of views. Whereas some members of the Options Generation simply regard sexual activity as one of the physical pleasures available to healthy young people, others regard it as something 'too special' to be engaged in lightly; still others feel that with the threat of AIDS and other sexually transmitted diseases hanging so heavily in the air, prudence and restraint is definitely called for.

And there might be another inhibiting factor at work: Professor Marita McCabe of Deakin University, reporting on a survey of sexual behaviour and attitudes among Australian adolescents, detects an emerging conservatism about sex which she attributes to a general caution about our economic and social future.[5] While the Boomers were experiencing economic buoyancy and social optimism (combined with pessimism about the threat of nuclear annihilation), they were impatient for sexual gratification. Professor McCabe may well be detecting the early signs of a significant shift: as the mood of the community darkens and young people begin to understand the long-term consequences of flat economic growth and sustained high unemployment, this may lead to greater hesitancy about making the kind of commitment involved in a serious sexual relationship.

There are still some signs of the age-old double standard operating in sexual matters. While virginity appears to have become less significant as a symbolic issue for young women, some young men can still be heard declaring that, in spite of the extent of their own sexual experience, they are determined to marry a virgin:

> *My brother is hopeless – he expects to have sex with any girl he takes out, but he keeps on saying that he wouldn't dream of marrying any of those girls. He still thinks you should marry a virgin.*

And, as one Boomer mother of a contemporary teenager put it:

> *Probably just as many girls are having sex as in our day. I just think they are more inclined to say that they are not virgins now, because that's what their friends are saying, or that's what's expected. It was the opposite in our day – you would say you were a virgin, even if you weren't.*

Because contemporary young people regard sex as being less of a 'big deal' than it used to be, they are somewhat bemused by the 'unhealthy interest' shown by Boomer parents in the sexual aspect of their children's relationships. Some report that their parents find it almost impossible to believe that close personal relationships with the opposite sex would not involve sexual activity; young adults themselves insist that sex does not dominate their relationships in the way it apparently did before *the group* eclipsed *the pair* as the social unit.

But some things never change:

It's all right to have sex if you really love someone . . . but first you have to know what love is. A lot of the guys you meet are just sex-crazy. As a matter of fact, I usually find I like a boy until I go out with him. I can't wait to go out with him and I think, 'This is going to be excellent', but when it comes to the day I think, 'Oh no! What am I going to do?' I just hate the thought of it.

While the female members of the Options Generation believe that their male friends are 'pretty well trained' in sexual etiquette, they are still subject to unwelcome and inappropriate attention from older men – especially in the workplace or in academic institutions. Young women report being discriminated against by men who are playing what the women see as 'a dangerous game' based on outmoded notions of sexuality and of appropriate behaviour between the sexes:

I think some men are even more aggressive now, because women have achieved so much. Sitting on the bus, you feel so vulnerable . . . this lecherous male gets on and you hope he isn't going to sit next to you. If they try anything, I just get up and move ostentatiously to another seat on the bus. People say that you are okay on trains at night because you should sit where the blue light is. That's where those sleazy guards are, though . . . that's the last place you'd go.

Discrimination is still rife. We were doing a project for one of our courses at TAFE where we were making videos. Believe it or not, the guys always got to work the cameras. It was unreal.

At my first job, I was sexually harassed and I didn't even realise. What he did to me was actually disgusting, but being so naive and stupid . . . well, he put it off as a joke, like, 'I'm just kidding'. The newsagent I used to work for was like that, too. Every day I went to work, I'd think, 'If you put your hands on me or say something' . . . but he would just laugh it off and say things

169

like, 'We're friends – we're practically family'. Then you would have to beg for your day off, and you never got paid on time.

The sense of being physically vulnerable is a continuing issue for young women – especially in large cities, and particularly at night. In spite of their feelings of personal power and liberation, they often express anxiety about their safety:

The big question is always whether you have enough money for a taxi. It can be a real power trip for men. We should all go and learn self-defence . . . a friend of mine had to fight off an attacker. After you've had a few nasty experiences, you soon learn . . .

Young women are more inclined than young men to regard themselves as victims of prejudice, sexual harassment, and discrimination. But there is another way in which young women may be victimised: the 'beauty myth' still has the power to generate body-centred neuroses which can lead to eating disorders:

I had the poor body-image thing when I was 18 and 19 and I virtually stopped eating. I would eat one meal a day – a big pile of boiled cabbage – and drink Diet Coke and water to put off feeling hungry. I went down to a size eight. People would say, 'You're looking a bit gaunt' and I'd think, 'Wow!' and I'd tell them what I'd been eating. I'd think, 'This is really cool'. I liked being told I was really silly.

Girls have to try much harder to be attractive than boys do . . . that's still an issue, as far as I am concerned. And then there are things like the cosmetic tax on tampons. You wouldn't find that if men had periods . . . there is actually still a lot of discrimination about, isn't there?

Discrimination is sometimes more trivial than that, but no less infuriating:

When I got my driving licence, the whole of the state of Victoria believed I was capable of driving by myself, but it took a long while before my parents would let me. But they let my brother drive the day after he got his licence.

And curfews are a much bigger thing with girls than with guys. I'm 20, and I still get the third degree: 'Where are you going? Who with?' Guys don't get that . . . not guys of my age.

Housework soon sorts out the degree of 'enlightenment' among young males, especially as judged by young females. Members of the Options Generation note that, even among the most ardently feminist mothers, there are still signs of an automatic tendency to assume that girls will do more domestic work – cooking, ironing, cleaning – than boys, and this creates difficulties when young males and females begin flatting together and negotiating the domestic arrangements. Things are changing rapidly in this area, but not rapidly enough for those women who believe that no vestige of gender stereotypes should be tolerated – especially if it is lurking in the male mind.

PIECES OF A PUZZLE

The Options Generation take pride in their individuality, their flexibility, their openness to possibility. They resist the idea of conformity and they hate generalisations being made about them.

Obviously, they are a generation who have had no alternative but to try to adapt to the changes taking place in the society in which they have spent their formative years. Some have been successful, and are facing early adulthood with confidence; some are still confused; some are alienated and depressed; some have already decided to withdraw from the struggle.

When members of the Options Generation plead to be regarded as individuals, they have a point: considering that the kaleidoscope of social change creates unpredictable patterns, the process of adaptation is bound to be highly individualistic. When the very character of a society is changing, it is hardly surprising that its young people will defy easy generalisations: they are the products of fragmentation, diversity and unpredictability. The fact that many of them wear the same fashions and adopt the same argot indicates nothing more than the fact that they – like all of us – are tribal creatures. But *in their minds*, they must deal with the challenge of trying to construct a framework for making sense of their own existence, when blueprints are not available, or are constantly being redrawn.

In 1996, the Australian Science, Technology and Engineering Council undertook a study of 15- to 24-year-olds. The ASTEC study focused primarily on young people's attitudes to technology. In reporting on the research, Richard Eckersley, a Canberra-based strategic analyst, wrote:

> Young people are not so much against science and technology; they acknowledge their importance in achieving a preferred future, and almost 70 per cent say science and technology offer the best hope for meeting the challenges ahead. But they are astute enough to realise science and technology are tools, and their impacts depend on who controls them and whose interests they serve.
>
> They expect to see new technologies used further to entrench and concentrate wealth and power: for example, they are almost twice as likely to believe that governments will use new technologies to watch and regulate people as they are [to believe] that new technologies will empower people and strengthen democracy.[6]

The importance of this research, according to Eckersley, is that it links young people's views on technology to their broader visions of a preferred future. The ASTEC study found that, for Australian young people:

> The belief that life will improve, nationally and globally, is a minority position. More than half believe that the 21st century

is more likely to be 'a bad time of crisis and trouble' than 'a new age of peace and prosperity'. Only one-third believe the quality of life in Australia will be better in 2010 than it is now.

Their dreams for Australia are of a society that places less emphasis on the individual, material wealth and competition, and more on community and family, the environment and coopera-tion. Some express their concerns in terms of a need for a greater recognition of the 'natural', 'human' or 'spiritual' aspects of life.

Such findings are congruent with young people's view of themselves as individuals who don't fit easily into conventional social cate-gories. But the pessimism emerging from Eckersley's research sug-gest that 'hanging loose' is not always the most comfortable position: postponing commitment might be a natural response to an uncertain and unstable world, but it can easily sap confidence.

Sooner or later, the sense of confidence which is fundamental to human motivation must come from some set of reference points which allow the individual to make sense of his or her life. In inter-preting his research among young people, Eckersley reminds us of the British historian Kenneth Clark's observation that 'it is lack of confidence, more than anything else, that kills a civilisation. We can destroy ourselves by cynicism and disillusion just as effectively as by bombs.'[7]

No one can yet say how the Options Generation will turn out, because we have yet to see which options they will exercise. There seems little doubt that most members of the Options Generation will ultimately marry and have children, and most will ultimately find work. But will the formative experiences which have already exerted a powerful influence on their lives cause them to be a rest-less and troubled generation? Will the fact that they have adapted as well as they have to the present rate of change equip them to cope, in the future, with a rate of change which will, presumably, continue to accelerate? Is their gloomy view of Australian society – that it lacks leadership, vision, and clear values – a reflection of an inner bleakness, or is it simply a clear-eyed, sceptical assessment by a generation of young realists?

When members of the Options Generation discuss their commitment to diversity, individuality and flexibility, they occasionally express the rueful thought that there is something missing: some of them envy earlier generations who had a more distinctive or coherent 'style' *(My mum was a teenager in the sixties . . . lucky thing!)*; some acknowledge that life might have been emotionally safer for people who lived at a time when religious belief and practice was more 'normal' than it is now; some wonder whether there was some foundation – in parenting or in education – available to earlier generations, but not to them.

Such concerns are fleetingly expressed, but they hint at a substratum of insecurity which is the Options Generation's response to what they see as the inherent uncertainty of their world – personal, national and global.

But words like 'insecurity' and 'uncertainty' aren't always interpreted in a negative way. Many members of the Options Generation are *proud* of their generation's ability to live in a fluid and hybrid culture: they might agree that the 1950s, 1960s and even 1970s had more obvious icons of popular culture (especially the culture of popular music) than have emerged in the 1990s, but so what? For a start, the lack of a strong, central idiom of pop culture has made it possible for the rampant individualists of the Options Generation to express themselves in more diverse and idiosyncratic ways. Pop culture, for them, is as kaleidoscopic as life itself. A multiplicity of musical styles, a multiplicity of bands, and even a multiplicity of new, do-it-yourself media outlets for youth culture are all signs of a fragmentation which, for those who are confident and energetic enough to thrive on it, feels like a healthy departure from the conformity of earlier generations.

In the field of rock music, Kathy Bail, a former editor of *Rolling Stone*, traces this trend towards fragmentation to the late 1970s and the early manifestations of punk rock. Bail's analysis of this phenomenon was that 'artists wanted to have a say in the way in which their music and art was produced and distributed' and, perhaps more importantly, they were reacting to 'boring, over-blown, stadium rock and corporate polish and control'.

Bail also identified the late 1970s as the era when fanzines – independent self-publications that rarely make a profit and are born out of a particular passion or obsession – came into their own: 'They are hand-made and photocopied and the content is generally raw, direct and uncensored'. Bail sees the emergence of 'zines as 'a further challenge to corporate culture and aims'.[8]

The leading edge of popular culture is one of the most reliable indicators of the emerging attitudes and values of the rising generation. The world of death metal and fanzines is not a world in which most members of the Options Generation live; it is just one of the myriad expressions of the emerging truth that this is a generation which is not just talking about non-conformity, but actually living life on its own terms, and accepting that those terms are themselves still evolving.

Some young people find all this too heady, too unpredictable and too rich for their blood. In response, they might resort to fundamentalist religion, or to the grey-suited security of the corporate world, or even to suicide. The point is that as members of the Options Generation, they know they are free to exercise whatever options they prefer, and they know that other members of their generation who have caught its essential truth will respect them for choosing whatever path they take and, indeed, for changing direction – however radically – whenever the time seems ripe.

Every generation in history draws comfort from its disapproval of the younger generation. The Options Generation have already started: from the heights of their late teens and early twenties, they are already capable of being quite scathing about those who are now entering their early and mid-teens:

> *It's all the little guys who are turning bad – the worst ones are under 18. If I was going to have a fist-fight, I wouldn't get involved with some of these younger kids. They are just as likely to pull a knife on you.*

I am wondering what is happening to the next generation – the way they talk, the way they spit in the street, the way they answer back. I am shocked at the language of some of the kids you hear on the train . . . it is as if they haven't got any discipline.

Kids who are finishing school now seem so much younger and less mature. You think to yourself, 'How could someone like him have his P plates?' Once you leave school, you seem to converse much better with people in their twenties.

One of the most vigorous criticisms of younger teenagers by members of the Options Generation is that they are in danger of slipping into a new cultural conformity, shaped by the idioms of the information revolution. The 'computer nerd' is classically seen as a young teenager who has been 'sucked in' by the Internet and whose language is punctuated by the jargon of information technology.

The rest of society might think that the Options Generation came through childhood and adolescence under the pressure of a burgeoning drug culture, a high rate of family breakdown, intense competition for university places and a generally discouraging labour market. To hear the Options Generation tell it, though, you would think that the pressures on the rising generation of teenagers are far more intense. (Some of them even take the benign view that the emerging 'conformism' of the generation coming after them is an understandable response to an increasingly hostile world.)

Perhaps, as the rate of change speeds up, the meaning of 'generation' is inevitably changing. The differences between the attitudes of ten-year-olds, 15-year-olds and 20-year-olds have always been apparent, but it has generally been assumed that, through most of history, such differences arose from different ways of looking at the same world. Today, those differences in intellectual and social maturity – and in the level of hormonal activity – are compounded by the fact that the world itself keeps changing.

5

INSECURITY MAKES
HUMANS OF US ALL

Australians of all generations share the view that 'you wouldn't want to live anywhere else'. Yet beneath that superficial optimism lurks a number of anxieties that are debilitating, and sometimes disabling. If diversity has become one obvious characteristic of Australian society, then insecurity is certainly another.

The high rate of youth suicide clouds every contemporary generation's view of Australian society. Associate Professor Pierre Baume, Director of the Australian Institute for Suicide Research and Prevention, has pointed out that Australia is the only country in the world with a peak suicide rate in people under 30 years of age, most of them male. In all other countries, suicide rates tend to rise with increasing age.

Although the statistics for both suicide and unemployment are sometimes interpreted in ways which may appear to exaggerate the size of the problem, both issues permeate the nation's consciousness. According to the Governor-General, Sir William Deane, youth unemployment is the most important issue facing us as a nation. At the opening of the 1997 National Convention of the Apex Clubs of Australia, Sir William said:

> Youth unemployment in contemporary Australia should not be
> seen as merely an economic problem to be evaluated as a factor

in some economic hypothesis and addressed only within the limits allowed by preconceptions of business efficiency. To the contrary, youth unemployment must be seen and addressed as an overwhelming social problem which is already having permanent destructive consequences with respect to the self-confidence, self-respect and self-esteem of a significant proportion of a whole generation of young Australians. It is a problem that should be in the forefront of the minds of all caring Australians all the time, until it is resolved.

In that regard, it is of great importance that our young people who are unable to obtain employment are not seen by others or by themselves as having somehow failed. The plain fact is that it is our society which has failed them.[1]

The uneasy sense of having somehow failed the rising generation is a significant contributor to the darkening mood of contemporary Australia, but each generation has its own litany of more specific insecurities as well.

The older generation feel anxious about the direction in which Australian society appears to be moving. They fear for the future of the institutions they have established. They are concerned about their grandchildren's welfare (not only in the labour market, but in a society which they believe will become even more fragmented, more violent and less compassionate than the one that they recall from 40 years ago or more). They also fear for their own physical safety and, even at this late stage, they still experience some anxiety about being old in a society which does not venerate age.

The Boomers attribute their insecurities to the stress caused by the relentless impact of social change, and the unexpected instability of their middle years. They expected *some* turbulence – after all, they were the architects and engineers of a new social order – but they assumed they would be in control of the revolution.

The Options Generation, for all their cool adaptability, often feel alienated and depressed by the bleakness of their prospects, the boredom of their lives, or the pressure exerted on them by the expectations of family, school or society at large. Their desire to escape regularly into oblivion – whether induced by extremely loud music, alcohol or hallucinogenic drugs – is a symptom of the same urge that drives some of them to suicide.

To say that we are all insecure might not be saying much more than that we are all human, since insecurity is part of the human condition. But even if our insecurities rise within us from a universal wellspring, they nevertheless feel as if they are uniquely ours; linked to the peculiar problems of this time and this place.

The emerging field of evolutionary psychology offers a view of contemporary Western (especially suburban) society which suggests that almost regardless of the specific ups and downs of recent social and economic change, we have simply not yet had enough time to adapt to the cataclysmic changes in our way of life wrought by the Industrial Revolution – changes which saw the population move from the relative security of life in a hunter-gatherer village to a very different life in the vast suburbs that sprang up around industrial towns and cities. The well-established rhythms of pastoral and agricultural life gave the inhabitants of a village the psychological comfort not only of living in a relatively stable extended family within the context of a relatively stable social network, but also the reassurance of living in direct relationship with the land that sustained them.

Suburban life, by contrast, is characterised by the fragmentation of extended families, the mobility of the population, the separation of work and home, and the removal of any direct sense of dependency on the land. In particular, the typical suburb has robbed us of one of our most precious cultural resources: the village square – the place where daily social contact created the glue that bound us into a community. Isolated in our suburban homes and apartments, coming and going in the sealed capsule of the motor car, we have paid a high emotional price for our material comfort. We have only recently tried to create suburban spaces where village life could be revived; places where we can eat, drink, shop, talk, walk and relax together.

According to evolutionary psychology, the process of adapting from village life to suburban life has been so disruptive to the human psyche that it will be many more generations before adaptation successfully occurs. In the meantime, the theory claims to account for widespread feelings of alienation, depression and other neuroses among the suburban population.

If that theory were to be our framework, we might expect that the Options Generation would be showing the healthiest signs of successful adaptation, and we might interpret the gap between them and their parents and grandparents as positive evidence of that process. But the rising rate of youth suicide challenges that interpretation and, in any case, the fact that we are now being overtaken by the Information Revolution might have already distorted the process of adapting to the social consequences of the Industrial Revolution.

Whether or not you choose to adopt that particular account of Western society's psychological problems, it does seem likely that a satisfactory explanation of contemporary generation gaps will not be found in the conventional view of a simple journey through the life cycle, but in a much bigger picture of social and cultural change.

Differences in attitude between the Lucky Generation, the Boomers and the Options Generation do not seem to be a function of mere maturation; they are signs of an emerging social reality in which the only certainty is *uncertainty*.

Perhaps our changing attitudes to marriage, parenthood, work and even the vexed question of our cultural identity are merely *symptoms* of a more radical shift towards acceptance of the idea that when we construct our own world-view, we are actually constructing our own reality as well. (Perhaps the marriage between subjectivity and relativity, celebrated by the Boomers, is being consummated by the Options Generation.) The 20th-century obsession with 'seeing is believing' appears to be yielding to the ancient, contrary view that 'believing is seeing'.

However we choose to interpret it, the rising generation are sending us a message from our future. If we are to bridge those infamous generation gaps, we shall have to find the courage to listen to what they are saying. That doesn't mean that we will enjoy or accept, let alone agree with, everything we hear. But if we are going to coexist harmoniously with each other in a shifting culture, we need to have some idea of the nature and direction of the shift (and, indeed, whether it is superficial and fleeting or profound and irrevocable).

CHANGING WORLDS, CHANGING WORLD-VIEWS

New experiences create new attitudes and values. As the divorce rate rises, for example, attitudes to the institution of marriage change. As life expectancy increases (from 1947 to 1995 it has increased by about ten years for both men and women), so attitudes towards old age inevitably change. But the changes don't stop there: an increase in life expectancy also affects our attitudes towards parenting and our choice of the moment when we will decide to have children. Even our attitudes towards marriage are affected by increased life expectancy. As divorces in middle age and later become more common, they are often explained in terms of marriages having 'run their course' or the belief that the very idea of lifelong partnerships is less realistic as life itself lasts longer.

The advent of the contraceptive pill changed attitudes not only towards sex and parenthood, but also towards abortion. The advent of the 'morning-after' pill further blurs the distinction between contraception and abortion.

New technologies ('smart cards', ATMs, robots in factories) change attitudes to work, leisure, money and shopping. The fast-food revolution changes attitudes to cooking, eating and nutrition. The widespread availability of mind-altering drugs changes attitudes to the 'recreational' use of drugs and to the legitimacy of the altered-reality states they induce.

One of the consequences of relentless social, cultural, economic and technological change, therefore, is that, in addition to the anxiety it provokes in many people, it challenges existing 'categories' we use for defining and interpreting our way of life.

The distinction between fiction and non-fiction is one very obvious manifestation of the blurring of traditional categories. As novelist Saul Bellow put it at a Yale University commencement ceremony in 1972, 'so much of narrative art has yielded itself to reportage'.[2] Tom Wolfe, widely regarded as the originator of 'the new journalism' would celebrate that blurring; the success of Helen Garner's *The First Stone,* a novelistic account of an actual event involving a sexual harassment case in a university college, indicates how readily the modern reader accepts a merging of art and reportage. In *The New Journalism*, Wolfe describes the declining status of the traditional novel and the rising status of non-fiction writing that uses the techniques of fiction:

> The novel no longer has the supreme status it enjoyed for 90 years (1875–1965), but neither has the New Journalism won it for itself. The status of the New Journalism is not secured by any means. In some quarters, the contempt for it is boundless . . . even breathtaking . . . With any luck at all the new genre will never be sanctified, never be exalted, never given a theology. I probably shouldn't even go around talking it up the way I have in this piece. All I meant to say when I started out was that the New Journalism can no longer be ignored in an artistic sense. The rest I take back . . . The hell with it . . . Let chaos reign . . . louder music, more wine . . . The hell with the standings . . . The top rung is up for grabs. All the old traditions are exhausted, and no new one is yet established. All bets are off! the odds are cancelled! it's anybody's ball game! . . . the horses are all drugged! the track is glass! . . . and out of such glorious chaos may come, from the most unexpected source, in the most unexpected form, some nice new fat Star Streamer Rockets that will light up the sky.[3]

The same kind of boundary shift is occurring in music. The conventional barrier between classical music and popular music begins to crumble as composers from both realms explore each other's territory (and, indeed, as new electronic media provide new ways of generating and blending sound). Younger performers and listeners accept an acceleration in the tempo at which 'classical' works are played; Bach is jazzed up; a Mozart symphony is given an electronic drumbeat and takes the pop charts by storm; Lennon and McCartney ballads are rearranged as baroque motets.

In politics and the mass media, as well, the community is basing its judgements on a changing set of criteria. The simple question 'Is this true?' is giving way to more subjective assessments of whether a person, a proposition or a news report is 'useful', 'entertaining' or 'convincing'. 'What's in this for me?' is becoming a more interesting question to the mass audience than the harsher alternative: 'Can I believe this?' (Recent qualitative research into Australian media consumers' reactions to the mass media confirms that as people come to recognise their own capacity for subjective interpretation, they gradually adopt a more sceptical attitude towards media presentations of 'facts' on the grounds that journalists, too, are likely to be just offering an opinion.)

That the mass audience could have moved to a position of using the mass media as a source of stimulation, entertainment and diversion without being too fussed about the precise distinction between news and opinion, looks like the sign of a significant cultural shift. Part of this shift involves a challenge to the traditional idea of *authority*: many radio listeners are just as impressed by the opinions of callers on talk-back radio as they are by the views of those identified as professional journalists or other 'experts'. (One of the consequences of more flexible cultural boundaries is that, increasingly, people will adopt the view that 'everyone's opinion is as valid as everyone else's'.)

The concept of multiculturalism is another symptom of the breaking down of traditional cultural barriers involving, as it does, a willingness to jettison ethnic stereotypes and to regard ethnicity as just another dimension of our diversity. The very concept of nationalism itself begins to change as we develop a stronger regional and global awareness, and acknowledge that our traditional, nation-based 'tribalism' answers a primitive but increasingly irrelevant need. Some of our tribal needs are already being met by our association with organisations and other communities which transcend or are disconnected from national boundaries.

When so many traditional categories no longer seem valid or attractive (or even begin to seem undesirably restrictive and prejudiced), other, more profound aspects of our thinking are likely to change as well. We begin to open our minds to some of the eternal philosophical puzzles, and to question some of the conventional distinctions we might previously have taken for granted: the distinction between the self and others, between the mind and the body, between ourselves and the world, between creators and their creations.

In an increasingly ambiguous and transitory culture, where conventional frameworks collapse and categories blur and merge, insecurity is bound to be heightened. For some people, this will be a spur to more creative and experimental approaches to everything from work to marriage. For others, the rise of relativism and the idea of more flexible boundaries will seem either threatening or simply silly: nothing more than a crazy outbreak of egocentricity and rampant subjectivity in which people have declared themselves free to 'make it all up as they go along'.

Allan Bloom, in *The Closing of the American Mind*, spoke for many older Australians as well when he exposed what he sees as the intellectual and moral confusions of our time. One of Bloom's central claims is that our contemporary passion for tolerance is a mere disguise for an unhealthy drift into relativism. He is particularly critical of the marriage of the drug culture with the contemporary music scene because he believes that it offers an ultimately unfulfilling short cut to the experience of ecstasy and gratification:

Rock music provides premature ecstasy and, in this respect, is like the drugs with which it is allied. It artificially induces the exultation naturally attached to the completion of the greatest endeavours – victory in a just war, consummated love, artistic creation, religious devotion and discovery of the truth. Without effort, without talent, without virtue, without exercise of the faculties, anyone and everyone is accorded the equal right to the enjoyment of their fruits. In my experience, students who have had a serious fling with drugs – and gotten over it – find it difficult to have enthusiasms or great expectations. It is as though the colour has been drained out of their lives and they see everything in black and white. The pleasure they experienced in the beginning was so intense that they no longer look for it at the end, or as the end. They may function perfectly well, but dryly, routinely. Their energy has been sapped, and they do not expect their life's activity to produce anything but a living, whereas liberal education is supposed to encourage the belief that the good life is the pleasant life and that the best life is the most pleasant life.[4]

Such assertions would make immediate sense to members of the Lucky Generation, and the views of people like Allan Bloom would be increasingly attractive to those Boomers who are searching for the ethos – in education, in religion, in morality – which they suspect was there but which they failed to embrace. To other Boomers and to many members of the Options Generation, however, statements like Bloom's would appear meaningless, since any pathway to ecstasy would be regarded as valid for those who take it, and dealing with the consequences will simply be part of the process of working out what to do next.

Our attitudes are both a response to the way in which the world is changing *and* a way of looking at the changing world. A generation growing up in a world of instability, uncertainty, impermanence and ambiguity will, inevitably, interpret that world quite differently from the way their parents and grandparents interpret it. Each of us uses our life's experiences, especially the experiences of our formative years, to spin a protective cocoon of values and beliefs. That cocoon, in turn, also serves as a kind of filter: we interpret situations and ideas we encounter in terms of the attitudes we have already formed. For this reason, it is often hard for us to understand that the world really is changing; that culture is an evolving thing; that the voice of the rising generation has some legitimate things to say to us.

But there are always some people who are intuitive or skilful enough to see what's coming. Often they are artists, sometimes critics, historians or philosophers. In the mid-sixties, Jacob Bronowski, author of *The Ascent of Man*, was anticipating the cultural upheavals to come. In an essay entitled 'Where do we go from here?', Bronowski wrote:

> It is evident that we are living in a cultural reformation – a harsh and perhaps disruptive movement in which we are all engaged. The fabric of western culture, its tangled skein of social habits, artefacts and values, is being pulled apart and made over – by us. We have set going the headlong changes in conduct and belief which now fill us with questions. Is there a single direction in these changes? Is there, in particular, an imaginative direction in the arts and sciences which points the way for a future culture? How shall we educate fresh generations, either to follow the changes or to lead them? What is the future of man? And is there any point in our wanting that future to conform to our own conception of man?[5]

That 'harsh and perhaps disruptive movement' has been felt most keenly by the Boomer generation who were coming to adulthood at the very time of Bronowski's reflections. It was they who opened the door to moral relativity, they who challenged the institutions of the day and they who set out to change the world by rewriting the rules.

One of the paradoxes of the Boomer generation is that their iconoclasm took place in the context of a comfortable, suburban, middle-class existence. They were able to embrace the politics of personal revolt with the support of full employment and material affluence. They could challenge everything and yet, in another sense, challenge nothing: they could talk and think in revolutionary ways, with the expectation of continued middle-class prosperity underpinning their non-conformist individualism. Their existentialist liberation from their parents' framework of values might have seemed heady and adventurous, but they still had their feet firmly planted on the same ground as their parents: the same jobs, the same material goals, the same desire for home and family on the same kind of quarter-acre block.

Some of the tension being carried by the Boomer generation may be the result of living with this inherent paradox. Perhaps more than they realised, they were living as their parents' children while *feeling* as if they had broken the mould. They wanted to please themselves; now they are not sure whether they have been pleased by what they have done (especially if they are still harbouring doubts about the quality of their parenting, or the integrity of their decision to divorce), and they are no longer even sure whether 'pleasing themselves' was such an estimable goal, after all.

This tension is heightened by their observation of the emerging attitudes and values of their children's generation. Many Boomers are torn between the competing attractions of their parents' sense of security and their children's sense of freedom. They know they rejected some of the rigidities and absolutes of their parents' worldview, but they are not sure whether they ever really wanted to move as far in the direction of flexibility as their children now seem to have gone.

Not surprisingly, many Boomers now find themselves in the mood to rethink their life's direction and to open themselves to values – religious, moral, social and cultural – which they thought they had safely rejected. The 'back to basics' movement, warmly applauded by the Lucky Generation, is actually a creature of the Boomers.

One of the great cultural revolutionaries of the 1960s, Richard Neville – co-publisher of the satirical *Oz* magazine and a vigorous opponent of censorship – has moved to the position where, faced by the new frontiers of violent pornography and the potential for 'psychic numbing' as a media effect, and conscious of the emotional vulnerability of his own daughters, he has been prepared to call for a clean-up of 'the garbage in our living rooms'. In *Out of My Mind*, Neville questions whether contemporary media content is 'life-enhancing or life-degrading'; whether it is 'defeatist, ignoble, sadistic, or empowering, illuminating, honourable'. 'I don't believe the media should be restrained because of a few vulnerable sad sacks,' Neville writes. 'My fear is this – that we may all be more vulnerable than we think.'

In a reflective postscript to *Out of My Mind*, Neville voices some thoughts which will reassure many Boomers who are struggling to find a moral focus:

> I admit to feeling ineffectual and isolated sometimes. I have an urge to warn the kids to on no account go the way I did – living on the fringe, yapping on the sidelines.[6]

Stephanie Dowrick, feminist publisher, writer and psychotherapist, tapped a rich vein of Boomer yearning with her 1997 book, *Forgiveness and Other Acts of Love*, in which she praised such traditional virtues as fidelity, restraint and generosity.[7] That followed another popular work, *The Book of Virtues*, edited by William J. Bennett, which presented a welcome 'treasury of moral stories' to people who were becoming conscious of their own uneasiness in the face of moral ambiguity.[8]

The likely success of both those books was presaged by an earlier, more whimsical response to the Boomers' quest for moral guidance. *Life's Little Instruction Book* by H. Jackson Brown offered '477 suggestions, observations, and reminders on how to live a happy and rewarding life', presented as a father's advice to his adolescent son, and became a worldwide bestseller.[9]

The Me Generation is having a massive rethink: some of them will turn, like Dowrick, to moral frameworks constructed out of ancient wisdom and a heritage which, in their earlier years, they might have regarded as unacceptably conservative, or even 'square'. Others, though, will continue to be destabilised by their inability to embrace either the idealism of their parents *or* the comprehensive cynicism of their children. For a generation priding themselves on their *freedom to choose*, this is turning out to be one of the toughest choices of their middle years.

Their parents, the Lucky Generation, were limited by life choices which seem, by today's standards, to have been quite restrictive, yet they offer no complaint: they report that they extracted whatever satisfaction they could out of the situation in which they found themselves, and they had no sense of needing to have more choice.

The Options Generation, raised on an endless array of choices, revel in the liberating sense that they can do anything they want. They are in no hurry to be committed to one direction or another, but remain comfortable with the idea of trying this, trying that; waiting and seeing how things will turn out. The freedom to make choices is such an integral part of their world that it is not a big issue for them.

Caught in the middle, the Boomers have had more choice than their parents, less choice than their children, yet they have been burdened by a sense of *needing* to choose, as though the satisfaction of their lives would depend on making the right choices. Some of the Boomers, especially Boomer women, are now beginning to wonder whether they have been obsessed by the notion of choice.

Perhaps it is not surprising, therefore, that in their middle years, the Boomers are becoming attracted to the idea of closing off some of their choices – moral and otherwise – partly in a quest for their parents' apparent sense of moral comfort, and partly because they are a little scared by the prospect of having to keep on making choices in the absence of a clear moral framework.

The Austrian psychiatrist Viktor Frankl, in *Man's Search for Meaning*, expressed a view which would chill the hearts of many Boomers who are starting to fear the consequences – for them and their children – of a life lived without moral purpose:

> No instinct tells him what he has to do, and no tradition tells him what he ought to do; sometimes he does not even know what he wishes to do . . . This existential vacuum manifests itself mainly in the state of boredom.[10]

LEARNING TO LIVE WITH AMBIGUITY

One of the potential hazards for a society trying to 'keep an open mind' – one which rates tolerance as being, perhaps, the highest of the virtues – is that it exposes itself to a heightened risk of manipulation.

This is one of the things that frightens the Lucky Generation, and growing numbers of Boomers, about the 'hang loose' and 'wait-and-see' approach of the Options Generation.

At a time when the previously dominant stories of Australian society – social, political, constitutional, cultural, religious, moral – are being re-examined, the question is: where will the new stories come from? Who will tell them? Who shall we believe?

At such a time, a society becomes vulnerable to the voices of demagogues who may expose our uncertainties and insecurities, but also to the carefully contrived stories of those with vested interests – in politics, commerce or a particular cultural perspective. The 'spin doctors' who painstakingly prepare every political utterance with an eye to its electoral consequences; the marketing strategists who by skilful creation of brand images construct the 'realities' of the marketplace; advocates and barrow-pushers of every kind have a greater opportunity of being heard when society's intellectual and moral frameworks have become more flexible.

In other words, our insecurities and uncertainties stimulate our desire for security and certainty: we are almost instinctively attracted to the confident voice; the strong leader; the person who seems to know what ought to be done. Moral vacuums yearn to be filled.

The danger, at such times, is that we might settle for an easy certainty, when uncertainty might be more appropriate; we might take refuge in the security of a simple view of the world, when the world might actually be more complex than we would wish.

These are challenging ideas to generations who have *not* grown up in an age of discontinuity. Every generation born in 20th-century Australia has, of course, lived through dramatic and life-changing upheavals in society. But it is only those born in the last 25 years or so who have never expected anything other than instability; who have factored uncertainty into their view of the world; who have assumed, from the beginning, that things would change constantly and rapidly.

Not all members of the Options Generation can thrive in this kind of environment, but their experience has clarified the challenge for the rest of us: not to turn back the clock; not to rail against the rate of change nor to ignore it, ostrich-like, in the hope that the storm will pass; not to devote too much time and energy to dreaming of ways to escape. The challenge is to learn how to live with uncertainty.

If our society is not inspired and encouraged to find new ways of adapting to the inherent instability of the modern world, we will continually fall back on unproductive strategies like over-regulation and fundamentalism in an attempt to 'restore order'. At a 1997 conference of artists and arts administrators, journalist and biographer David Marr remarked that 'when government gives in to calls for censorship, the pressure for censorship builds. Intelligent government knows when to turn a deaf ear.'[11] Marr was acknowledging that in the realm of censorship – as in every other realm of life – to fall victim to our insecurities is to risk stifling our aesthetic judgement and moral sensitivity.

But there is another alternative. Knowing that the world is an unpredictable and uncertain place, we could learn to accept that, rather than resisting it or pretending it isn't true. Knowing there is inherent instability in the process of social and cultural development, we could train ourselves to cope with inconsistency, contradiction and even ambiguity.

This is not the mighty challenge it might first appear to be. We all live, already, in a world of contradictions. Almost without exception, we experience flashes of hatred for the people we love most. (How can that be? It can easily be, because we are not always rational; we are merely human.) We can desperately want to live simpler lives, even while we continue to complicate them. We can espouse the ideal of spending more time with our family and friends, nurturing our relationships, while structuring our lives in a way which effectively guarantees that less time will be available to spend in that way.

We are perfectly capable of whingeing and grumbling incessantly about the state of Australian society, while passionately defending Australia as 'the best country on earth'. At election time, we can subscribe to the view that a new leader will save us and then, 18 months later, resort in despair to the cliché that 'all politicians are hopeless'.

Generationally, we do the same thing. The Lucky Generation take pride in the quality of their parenting, yet offer quite scathing criticisms of the way their children have turned out.

The Boomers seem able to worry, simultaneously, about their over-parenting *and* the lack of time they are able to devote to their children. They say they only wanted their children to be happy, yet they admit that they probably put them under too much pressure. They wish their children were not so materialistic, yet they find themselves overindulging them.

The Options Generation carry their own cultural contradictions: they complain that their generation lacks a cultural focus, or a clearly established set of 'icons' while, at the same time, expressing pride in their *lack* of iconic focus.

None of this should amaze us. Each of us spins, in the intimate recesses of our own psyche, a complex web of inconsistent attitudes, values and beliefs. The challenge is to take what we know to be true in private and apply it to the external world. The world is not a place where social, cultural, economic or technological change moves in straight lines, or in consistent patterns, or at a steady rate. The world is a place where contradictory influences produce unpredictable outcomes.

Peter O'Connor, the Melbourne psychotherapist and author of *Understanding the Mid-Life Crisis*, said in an interview published in the *Good Weekend* magazine:

> To me, the whole art of that second half of life is to begin to not know . . . Our culture mistakenly thinks that knowledge and wisdom are the same things, but real growth comes in the feeling life, in the inner life, by being able to tolerate uncertainty and ambiguity long enough to find out what it is that you need to know.[12]

Many members of the rising generation are acknowledging that they had better not allow their ego to become too involved in their plans; otherwise, when the plans inevitably have to change, the ego will be too easily bruised. Their way of dealing with unpredictability is to expect the unexpected and to try to build their confidence and self-esteem out of something other than this course of study, that job, or even a friendship which may or may not endure. Growing up in an age of uncertainty, young people inevitably make the painful discovery that security is an internal state which can only be constructed out of an internal set of values.

If our sense of security is constructed out of expectations of how other people will act, or how the world will treat me, or what the next economic cycle will bring, the structure will inevitably crumble. Perhaps the Options Generation have already learned something that their parents are struggling to articulate: that life must be lived fully in the present, and that plans for the future should be lightly drawn.

Whether the emerging outlook of the Options Generation is a sign of a true culture-shift, or whether it is a more temporary indication of their short-term response to the rate of socio-economic change, the deeper message is clear: the rising generation, *and* their parents, *and* their grandparents have all come out of a society which is itself in a state of transition. The three generations represent three phases of that transition, with many more yet to come.

Moral frameworks are powerful indicators of these different phases. The Lucky Generation believe that they acquired a clear set of values from their parents (and from their own childhood experience) which has remained intact throughout their lives, and which has served them well as a resource for making sense of their lives. In their view, if rising generations (and, indeed, immigrants) don't share those traditional values, then more rules and regulations will need to be imposed on society to ensure that people will 'behave themselves'.

The Options Generation, on the other hand, have grown up with the idea of flexible moral boundaries: they create and re-create moralities out of their more complex ways of relating to each other, and they are comfortable with a greater degree of flexibility than their parents or grandparents can easily tolerate. (To many of them, the notion of moral absolutes would seem as alien as the idea of rigid gender distinctions.)

Between these two extremes, the Boomers have tried to make sense of lives generally lived outside their parents' moral framework. They are only now showing signs of wanting to re-examine that framework and even, belatedly, to adopt it as a resource for interpreting the world to their children.

There is no reason why the three generations should see the world in the same way, nor is there any probability that they will. Progress towards harmonious coexistence depends on our acknowledging that each of us is a product of the society which shaped us and that homogeneity, if it ever existed, is a thing of the past.

After all, the increasing complexity of Australian society is only a reflection of the increasing complexity of our lives and our identities. One of the many outcomes of the gender revolution is that we have become more conscious of the fact that multiple roles really amount to multiple identities: our sex, marital status, family relationships, work and social groups, and even our passions, each define only part of us.

Australian society is no different from that. We are many different people – ethnically, culturally, economically, politically, and generationally. Yet we are one society. Our greatest challenge is to discover the core values that define our essence and give unique meaning to the word 'Australian'.

NOTES

INTRODUCTION
1. D. M. Thomas, *Eating Pavlova* (London: Sceptre, 1995), p. 6.

CHAPTER 1
THREE GENERATIONS: THREE AUSTRALIAS?

1. The *Australian,* 28 July 1997.
2. Kathy Bail, 'Do It Yourself Feminism', *The Sydney Papers,* vol. 9, No. 7 (The Sydney Institute, Summer 1997), p. 2.
3. Julie Martin, quoted in Kathy Bail, op. cit., p. 9.
4. Erica Jong, *Fear of Fifty* (London: Vintage, 1994), pp. 246–7.
5. H. J. Eysenck et al. (eds), *Encyclopedia of Psychology,* vol. 2 (London: Search Press, 1972), p. 15.

CHAPTER 2
BORN IN THE 1920s: THE 'LUCKY' GENERATION

1. Michael Cannon, *The Human Face of the Depression* (Mornington: Today's Australia Publishing Company, 1996), p. 18.
2. Geoffrey Blainey, 'Turning Point: How the Forties Changed Us Forever', the *Australian Magazine,* 12–13 October 1996, p. 18.
3. J. B. Chifley, quoted in Geoffrey Blainey, op. cit., p. 18.
4. Geoffrey Blainey, op. cit., p. 17.
5. Geoffrey Blainey, op. cit., pp. 16–7.
6. Michael Cannon, op. cit., p. 137.
7. Ronald Conway, 'Let's Hear It for the Forgotten Decade', the *Australian Magazine,* 22–23 February 1997, p. 27.
8. Donald Horne, *The Lucky Country: Australia in the Sixties* (Ringwood: Penguin Books, 1964), p. 239.
9. David Thomson, quoted in Sally Loane and Paul Cleary, 'Generation Exposed', the *Sydney Morning Herald,* 12 April 1997.

10. Alan Tapper, 'The Welfare Culture of Confusion', Bert Kelly Lecture no. 10 (Perth: Centre for Independent Studies, 1993), p. 3.

CHAPTER 3
POSTWAR BABY BOOMERS: THE 'STRESS' GENERATION

1. Gordon Carmichael, *With This Ring* (Canberra: Department of Demographic Studies, Australian National University, and Australian Institute of Family Studies, 1988), p. 206.
2. Professor Alf Pollard, quoted in Tony Stephens, 'The 60s: Another Country', the *Sydney Morning Herald,* 8 June 1997.
3. Philip Ruthven, quoted in Debra Jopson and Greg Lenthen, 'Baby Boomers: Who'll Pay When They're Grey?', the *Sydney Morning Herald,* 12 July 1994.
4. Rob Keavney, quoted in Debra Jopson and Greg Lenthen, op. cit.
5. Susan Oliver, quoted in Debra Jopson and Greg Lenthen, op. cit.
6. Arun Abey, quoted in Debra Jopson and Greg Lenthen, op. cit.
7. Reg Bryson, quoted in Neil Shoebridge and Adele Ferguson, 'Rise of the Baby-Boom Bosses', *Business Review Weekly,* 20 January 1997, pp. 29, 34.
8. Neil Shoebridge and Adele Ferguson, op. cit., p. 34.
9. Naomi Woolf, *Promiscuities* (Sydney: Random House, 1997), quoted in *Good Weekend,* 10 May 1997, p. 23.
10. Dr Don Edgar, 'How the Baby Boom Backfired', the *Bulletin,* 29 January–5 February 1991, p. 148.
11. Jo-Ann Goodwin, 'The New Man: Toxic Waste of Feminism', the *Guardian,* reprinted in the *Sydney Morning Herald,* 18 February 1993.
12. Erica Jong, op. cit., p. 139.
13. Diana Bagnall, 'Altered Images', the *Bulletin,* 16 April 1996, p. 19.
14. Walter Truett Anderson, *Reality Isn't What It Used To Be* (New York: HarperCollins, 1990), p. 192.

15. Deborah Hope, 'The Age of the Hyper Parent', the *Weekend Australian*, 19–20 July 1997.
16. Deborah Jackson, *Do Not Disturb* (London: Bloomsbury Publishing, 1994), quoted in Deborah Hope, op. cit.
17. Wendy Cohen, quoted in Deborah Hope, op. cit.
18. Steve Biddulph, quoted in Mike Safe, 'Boys To Men', the *Australian Magazine*, 2–3 August 1997, p. 14.
19. Ross Gittins, 'Middle Class Takes Stock', the *Sydney Morning Herald*, 23 July 1997.

CHAPTER 4
BORN IN THE 1970s: THE 'OPTIONS' GENERATION

1. Walter Truett Anderson, op. cit., pp. 155–6.
2. Sally Loane, 'The Big Business of Caring for Little Kids', *Good Weekend*, 17 August 1997, p. 33.
3. Gay Ochiltree and Don Edgar, quoted in Sally Loane, op. cit., p. 31.
4. Quentin Bryce, quoted in Sally Loane, loc. cit.
5. Professor Marita McCabe, quoted in the *Sydney Morning Herald*, 5 February 1997.
6. Richard Eckersley, 'Modern Youth's Angst', the *Weekend Australian*, 7–8 September 1996.
7. Kenneth Clark, quoted in Richard Eckersley, op. cit.
8. Kathy Bail, op. cit., p. 1.

CHAPTER 5
INSECURITY MAKES HUMANS OF US ALL

1. Sir William Deane, quoted in the *Sydney Morning Herald*, 11 July 1997.
2. Saul Bellow, quoted in Tom Wolfe, *The New Journalism* (London: Picador, 1975), p. 9.
3. Tom Wolfe, op. cit., pp. 50–1.
4. Allan Bloom, *The Closing of the American Mind* (New York: Simon & Schuster, 1987), p. 80.

5. Jacob Bronowski, 'Where Do We Go From Here?' in *A Sense of the Future* (Cambridge, Massachusetts: The MIT Press, 1977), p. 155.

6. Richard Neville, *Out of My Mind* (Ringwood: Penguin Books, 1996), pp. 78–9.

7. Stephanie Dowrick, *Forgiveness and Other Acts of Love* (Ringwood: Penguin Books, 1997).

8. William J. Bennett (ed.), *The Book of Virtues* (Melbourne: Bookman Press, 1993).

9. H. Jackson Brown, Jr., *Life's Little Instruction Book* (Melbourne: Bookman Press, 1991).

10. Viktor Frankl, *Man's Search for Meaning* (New York: Simon & Schuster, 1985), p. 106.

11. David Marr, 'Beware the New Age of Censorship', the *Sydney Morning Herald*, 4 December 1996.

12. Peter O'Connor, quoted in Alan Close, 'Homeless in the Heart', the *Weekend Australian*, 9–10 March 1996.

ACKNOWLEDGEMENTS

In the writing of *Generations* – and in my work as a researcher – my overwhelming debt is to the survey participants who willingly give their time and allow their privacy to be invaded by people like me.

Every day of the year, thousands of Australians agree to take part in face-to-face interviews, telephone interviews, mail surveys and group discussions being conducted by the many organisations who comprise the social research industry (including academics, government enterprises and commercial market research firms).

There is an indirect reward for participation in this vast and continuous research activity: people who agree to be interviewed, or to take part in group discussions, may derive some satisfaction from knowing they are contributing to a significant body of knowledge about the Australian way of life. But perhaps there is a more direct, personal reward as well: most participants in social research projects seem to enjoy the experience and are pleased to be consulted about their attitudes and beliefs. Nevertheless, I am conscious of the fact that no research of this kind could ever be conducted without the cooperation of the general public and although there is an increasing refusal rate among people who are approached to take part in research projects, the generosity of our respondents continues to be our most precious resource.

Special thanks are also due to my research colleagues – Elizabeth Turnock, Prue Parkhill and Margie Beaumont – who work with me on *The Mackay Report*, the long-term program of social research from which most of the data for *Generations* has been drawn.

The Mackay Report is funded by annual subscriptions from commercial and government organisations, and I am grateful to all those subscribers who, since 1979, have supported the program.

Finally, I wish to acknowledge a quite different kind of debt. In

attempting to synthesise some of my research into a broader picture
of Australian society, I have been particularly encouraged by the
example of three men: Phillip Adams, Donald Horne and Paul
Kelly.

For more than 40 years, Phillip Adams has been writing news-
paper columns about every aspect of Australian social, cultural and
political life, and I admire his boundless capacity for astute and
idiosyncratic analysis.

Donald Horne's first book, *The Lucky Country*, was published
at a time when many of the culture shifts documented in *Generations* were just beginning to become discernible. It still stands as an
exemplary work of social comment.

Paul Kelly's *The End of Certainty* created the definitive framework for making sense of Australia's struggle to come to terms with
cultural and economic discontinuity.

APPENDIX: The Research

Generations is based on the following 14 reports, each published as part of *The Mackay Report*, a continuous program of qualitative social research established in 1979 and funded by subscriptions from government and commercial organisations. (In the 19 years to date, a total of 89 *Mackay Reports* have been published.)

Being 19 Now (1980)
Retirement (1981)
Turning 40 (1985)
Turning 55 (1987)
Teenagers & Their Parents (1988)
Men & Women (1989)
The Family – '90s Style (1991)
The Grey Market (1993)
The Middle Years (1993)
DINKs (1994)
Young Adults (1995)
Men in the '90s (1995)
Born After the Boom (1997)
Mind & Mood (1997)

THE QUALITATIVE RESEARCH METHOD

In social research, it is critically important to find a method which is compatible with the things we are trying to investigate. For example, if we want to know how many people visit a particular place, or how much money they spend, or what they do while they are there, then a method which relies primarily on observation will be most appropriate. We can attach precise numbers to all those things, and so our data will be *quantitative*.

If we can't directly observe what people are doing, we may have to rely on an indirect research method, such as a questionnaire-based survey, to get an approximate idea of their behaviour based on their own recollections of what they did. Again, this information will be expressed in numbers, though the data will be less reliable than that obtained by direct observation.

If we want to determine the extent to which certain information is known within the community (for example, Australia's major exports, or the interest rates being charged by banks on home loans, or the policies of the major political parties on a particular issue), we can try to measure the extent of that knowledge by means of a structured questionnaire carefully designed to elicit people's awareness and recollection of the information.

But when we venture beyond the realm of behaviour and people's knowledge of relatively simple information into the more complex and subtle question of *why* people behave as they do, or how they *feel* about something – the area of attitudes, motivations, values and beliefs – the task is not so straightforward. Although research is sometimes undertaken to 'measure' attitudes, it generally takes the form of asking people a series of questions about their attitudes. In such cases, serious difficulties arise. For a start, every time you ask a question you are likely to receive an answer, and it is tempting to believe that the answer has told you what you wanted to know. But one of the hazards of attitude research based on structured questionnaires is that we can never be sure whether the answer was obtained only because the question was asked: does that 'attitude' or 'opinion' really exist, or does it only exist in the form of an answer to that question? Does it exist only *because* the question was asked?

The matter is further complicated by the fact that if we ask the same set of questions in a different order, we usually obtain different responses. If we vary the wording of the questions, the answers also vary. Researchers know that it is not hard to determine the outcome of a survey by controlling the way in which questions are asked. So what is the 'correct' form of any set of questions designed to reveal the attitudes we want to investigate, and what is the 'correct' order in which those questions should be asked? We can experiment with variations, but we can never be sure that we have eliminated the influence of questions on the answers we obtain. (One solution, as we shall see, is to avoid asking questions altogether – hence the development of so-called 'non-directive' research methods.)

There's another problem as well: when a set of structured questions is used to investigate attitudes, we can never be sure whether there are other attitudes present in our respondents' minds which lie beyond the scope of the questions. What *else* do people feel about a particular subject which we may have failed to discover because we didn't ask enough questions – or the right questions?

Questions involving the use of 'Why?' are a particular hazard in surveys based on a formal structured questionnaire. As soon as someone is asked 'Why?' about anything, the expectation is created that there *should* be a reason for the behaviour or the attitude under investigation. Once the expectation has been created that a 'reason' exists to explain some piece of behaviour, the respondent is likely to offer a rational-sounding response (which may be a mere rationalisation) in order to satisfy the rational demands of the question. 'Why did you buy that car?' 'Why did you stop going to church?' 'Why did you vote for that candidate?' All such questions assume that there's a reason for doing those things, yet we do many things for no 'reason' at all (at least, for no logical or easily explained reason).

In fact, one of the controversies in social research arises from the question of whether some attitudes, beliefs and values are appropriate for measurement at all. Measurement is a rational process, after all, so research instruments which are designed to obtain measurements are perfectly appropriate for rational data (how much? how often? when? where?). But if the *explanations* of behaviour are not rational, then why try to measure them? Even if some apparently simple and straightforward attitudes are measurable, the explanation of why those attitudes are held may not be.

Some social research sets out to quantify the *extent* to which people hold certain attitudes (or, more accurately, the extent to which they agree or disagree with statements which are thought to express those attitudes), but there are still serious problems involved in first trying to uncover the attitudes in question, and then trying to express them in a measurable form. It can be done, but it is a very complex process – generally involving finding a number of *different* ways of expressing each of the attitudes being investigated, until a more realistic, multi-dimensional 'picture' of the attitude emerges.

But even then, the fundamental issue remains: might it not be possible that people have attitudes or beliefs which are not capable of being measured? Isn't it possible that the rational instrument of a structured questionnaire is an inappropriate method for investigating information which may be non-rational and highly emotional in character? Might it not be more appropriate to devise a research method which is itself non-rational, non-linear and non-structured, in order to match more closely the nature of the material being investigated?

It is that kind of concern which led to the development of qualitative research methods. Because qualitative research is primarily concerned with explanation and diagnosis, the question of measurement hardly arises. Can we measure the happiness of a child at a party? The security of a loving relationship? The ambition of a school leaver? The despair of unemployment? The private pain of divorce? All these things can be explored and understood, but trying to measure them may be an inappropriate goal. Not everything that is 'real' or 'true' is necessarily quantifiable.

Qualitative research sets out to investigate attitudes, values and beliefs without the use of structured survey techniques designed to produce numbers. Qualitative research is deliberately designed to bypass the rational; to avoid the use of direct questions, especially those questions involving 'Why?'; to minimise any pressure on survey respondents to give answers which fit a particular survey instrument. (We still want to discover why, but experience suggests that there are better ways of doing that than asking the direct question.)

A doctor will generally use qualitative data (such as a conversation with the patient, or some insight into the patient's history and circumstances) to help interpret quantitative data from medical tests, before deciding on a diagnosis and prescribing some treatment. In the same way, qualitative social research is intended to illuminate our understanding of why people behave as they do. The best use of qualitative research is to explain some phenomenon which has already been established. (For example, quantitative measures of voting intention may reveal that electoral support for a government has slumped: qualitative research may be required to explain the reasons behind the slump, or to diagnose the mood of the electorate.)

The Mackay Report is based on two qualitative research techniques – group discussions and individual interviews – in an attempt to explain people's behaviour by exploring their underlying attitudes, values and beliefs in all their subtlety and complexity, without attempting to impose measurement on the exploration, and without asking any direct questions at all.

Non-directive group discussions and unstructured personal interviews

The group discussion technique involves taking the members of a natural, existing social group (typically five to eight friends, neighbours or work-mates) and arranging for them to meet together in their natural habitat (the home of one of them, or a workplace, or wherever the group feels most comfortable) to engage in relaxed, informal and unstructured discussion about the topic in question. No questions are asked; no formal agenda is set. The researcher plays no active part in the discussion, beyond an introduction which explains the purpose of the study, outlines the topic and describes the way in which the discussion might proceed.

Thus, in the relaxed and permissive atmosphere of a group of people who already know each other and are used to talking to each other, the discussion ranges widely over all aspects of the subject which interest or concern the members of the group. Some people will talk a great deal; others will say very little. The discussion will proceed as any natural, normal group discussion proceeds. There will be leaders and followers; those who are dominant and those who are submissive; agreements and disagreements; side-tracking and wise-cracking.

In the ebb and flow of natural conversation, the attitudes, values and beliefs of the group will gradually emerge. It is the dynamics of non-directive group interaction which yield the information we are seeking.

In order to be successful as a method for social research, the group discussion technique must have three features: the group must be a *real* group (that is, people who are well known to each other and who are used to interacting with each other); the discussion must be conducted on the home ground of the group – a place where it is natural for them to be, and where they feel most comfortable; the discussion must proceed freely and spontaneously, without any interference or any structure being imposed upon it by the researcher.

Of course, the group discussion technique has its limitations. It is not a suitable technique for eliciting information from people who are generally isolated from social interaction, and it is not suitable for eliciting the kind of information which people may not wish to discuss even in the company of friends with whom they are socially at ease. For these reasons, a comprehensive social research project must also employ another technique which overcomes these difficulties.

The Mackay Report uses, as its second technique, the unstructured (or 'in-depth') personal interview. This technique has a similar purpose to the group discussion, except that it involves a private conversation between researcher and respondent. Again, the interview takes place on the 'home ground' of the respondent; again, direct and formal questions are avoided; again, the respondent is encouraged to ruminate freely about the subject under review.

An important feature of both techniques is that the respondents' anonymity is guaranteed: although the information they give us is incorporated into our reports (often appearing – as in *Generations* – as verbatim quotations to illustrate or support our findings), the source of that information is kept absolutely confidential.

The information yielded by the non-directive group discussion and the unstructured interview technique is subjected to extensive and rigorous qualitative analysis procedures which are in every way as strict as those employed for the statistical analysis of quantitative research data, but follow quite different principles.

Because of the nature of qualitative methodology and the aims of the research (often to explore the *reasons* why people behave as they do), samples for qualitative social research are generally smaller than for quantitative surveys where the data will be subjected to routine statistical processing. Because the emphasis is on diagnosis and explanation, rather than measurement, we concentrate on the *diversity* of the sample (rather than its sheer size), so that each study incorporates the widest possible range of respondents within the practical limits of the project. (The structure and size of the sample varied for each of the 15 reports on which *Generations* is based: individual reports contain sample details.)

The fundamental rule is that each group and individual interviewee should be as different as possible from every other group and interviewee in the study in terms of such characteristics as sex, socio-economic status, position in the life cycle, geographical location and so on. In data analysis, one of the primary aims is then to discern the *range* of attitudes – the variations – emerging from that highly diverse sample.

In the end, of course, the integrity of social research – whether quantitative or qualitative – depends upon the interpretation of the data. All research is flawed, partly because there is no such thing as perfect interpretation, and partly because of the ever-present danger of the dreaded 'experimental effect': the possibility always exists that the information we are trying to interpret has been influenced by the methods we used to obtain it. One reason for our heavy reliance on the group discussion technique is that, when it is carefully applied, it seems to minimise the dangers of the 'experimental effect' by providing a method of data collection which is as *natural* as we can make it. As a further safeguard against misinterpretation, the continuous nature of this research program allows us to set the data from each individual study in the context of the broad sweep of the whole program. Our reliance on the team approach (with three or four researchers working independently on each project) further minimises the possibility of subjective bias in our analysis.

INDEX

Hugh Mackay
WHY DON'T PEOPLE LISTEN?

In *Reinventing Australia*, Hugh Mackay told us about ourselves as a society coming to terms with the impact of social change. Now, in *Why Don't People Listen?*, he gets personal.

It is easy to forget that our personal relationships are our most precious resource for coping with life in unstable and uncertain times. What we most need is each other.

When changes in society threaten to isolate us and rob us of the time we need for maintaining and nurturing our relationships, the big challenge is to become more effective communicators. In *Why Don't People Listen?*, Hugh Mackay shows us a simple yet revolutionary way to improve the quality of our relationships – at home or at work – through a more disciplined and sensitive approach to communication. Along the way, he identifies the ten most basic 'laws' of human communication.

WHY DON'T PEOPLE LISTEN? IS ONE OF THE MOST IMPORTANT BOOKS YOU WILL READ.

AVAILABLE FROM PAN MACMILLAN